It seems like yesterday . . .

$\mathcal{L}$ilacs two

the 1950s

by DAROLD 'DICK' FREDRICKS

Cover photo: Dick Fredricks, Dick Merrill, Bob Walton in Montana getting
ready for the 1956 Augie football season. D.E. Fredricks collection
Title photo: 1956 air photo of Augustana College; photo courtesy Center for
Western Studies

D.E. Fredricks
PO Box 733
San Bruno, CA 94066

LCCN: 2001118172

ISBN: 1-57579-230-3

Printed in the United States of America
PINE HILL PRESS
4000 West 57th Street
Sioux Falls, S.D. 57106

This book is dedicated to the memory of
Coach Bob Burns

Special thanks to my wife Peggy Fredricks

Table of Contents

LILAC *n.* Bluish (indigo) dark blue, indigo; any group of hardy shrubs or trees with large clusters of tiny, fragrant flowers—ranging in color from white, through many shades of lavender, to deep crimson.

Webster New World Dictionary 1962

—or any group of hardy people, with large clusters of tiny, fragrant children—ranging in size from small to large.

Fredricks family at Seventeenth Street/Eighth Ave. 1935: Back row children: Dorothy, Norman and Dick. Front row children: June, Charles and Jimmy

Introduction

In 1990, I retired after thirty years of teaching in California schools. I began returning in the spring and fall to the Heartland for visits. I felt I had missed out on a lot in the many years that I had been away working in California and I began looking for my roots. At my sister Dorothy's house in West Sioux, I began writing down the many experiences that I had during my first twenty-five years while growing up in Sioux Falls. It was like returning to a museum that had been locked up in my mind. When I began writing my thoughts, these vignettes, I guess I was trying to express the ultimate book, one that put me into the time frame of what I wanted to re-experience, sort of a virtual-reality or time machine concept. You could be there and experience the feel of the time and maybe be able to fill in some of the gaps. There are too many gaps in our memories. Too many names have been forgotten. The pictures are out of focus and the gaps need to be filled. Life is like that. We remember a few things, the pleasurable things. Much of the other basic things, the things that we think are routine are often what influence us the most and build our character: church, schools, buildings, people we see only occasionally, people we grow intimate with, places we visit, games we play. They are often times pushed beneath the surface of our minds and can only be regained when we get older and have the time to remember. Remember and analyze. That's what I've tried to do.

However, thoughts are not always continuous. They come to you in bits and pieces. These thoughts can be side-tracked so easily and end up so very far from where we want to be. Bits and pieces.

As I wrote my stories and thoughts down while in the back yard in West Sioux, I began to realize how many people had helped and guided me in my search for identity as I grew up. At the time I thought I was doing everything by myself, but that was due to my immaturity. I realized, for example, that Coach Bob Burns had a great deal to do with my success as a person. His style of coaching encouraged me to explore myself and put forth my best effort in all things.

Over my thirty years of teaching, I related many of these stories and thoughts to my students in California. It didn't take long before I realized what a wonderful foundation I had received in the Heartland on which to build my adult life. I also realized that the stories that I was telling were in actuality parts of a process that almost every child goes through while growing up and 'finding himself'. I, however, experienced an additional part of life that others my age seldom experience: my mother died when I was only eleven years old. During the troubled interlude after she died, I had to sort out the important things I had been taught in order to make decisions by myself and succeed in life. I did that, but in the process I experienced a lot of personal pain. In the long run, I adjusted. No more can be expected.

In 1999, I published many vignettes of my early life in Sioux Falls in a book, *When Lilacs Were in Bloom*. This book traced my struggle with growing up during the Depression. The stories were real life experiences with many morals to be learned from them. I was delighted with the reception it received from my many friends. I was surprised at the number of people who remembered me. I felt, however, that this book was only half of the story I wanted to tell. I had lived for twenty-five years in Sioux Falls, graduated from Washington High School, and my life to that point accounted for only eighteen years. My life and experiences were not complete and my football coach in high school, Bob Burns, was to play a second important part in my life. Success in football in high school was followed by humiliating football defeats at Augustana College. I continued to strive to find my identity in the world. After utter disillusionment, I left Augustana to attend Kansas University before I was drafted into the Army. I needed to finish the story of my college years and my stint in the Army during the Korean War. Coach Burns and Augustana would become a dominating influence in molding my life in 1956.

This book, *Lilacs Two, the 1950's* is the rest of the story.

Although many of the conversations in this book did occur, total recall of conversations by me was not possible so I took much liberty while writing them for this book. I hope nobody takes offense from them.

1
The Black Hills to Sioux Falls

Suddenly the pilot's voice on the airplane speaker startled me out of my thoughts—"Mount Rushmore can be seen below on the right of the plane. Take a look at our Citadel of Democracy."

We had been crossing over the Black Hills and I had been day-dreaming about Uncle Bill's ranch in Montana, but I quickly looked out to see the four gigantic heads of our past presidents of the United States carved into the granite mountain. The stark white color of the granite surprised me at first. It was so bright, but then I remembered that it had only been completed in the early 40s, a short time, geologically speaking. The shine hadn't worn off yet. The view was spectacular and sobering. Here I was, me, getting a view of the shrine that very few of the millions of visitors a year get to experience. It was awesome from the air. The heads seemed a lot smaller from the air. This domed granite up-thrust rock of the 6000 foot Harney Range in the Black Hills became the choice of Gutzon Borglum in the 1920s when he decided to carve a tribute to democracy using the Presidents George Washington, Thomas Jefferson, Abraham Lincoln, and Theodore Roosevelt as his subjects to represent all of the good in our country. Gutzon Borglum's family epitomized the movement of the pioneers when his family trekked 900 miles from Missouri to 'New Zion' by Utah's Great Salt Lake in the 1800s. He never forgot his western roots when he chose South Dakota to represent America's Shrine of Democracy.

As this domed granite rock quartet disappeared from sight, the hogback ridges of sandstone on the edge of the Black Hills came into view. The Black Hills were formed like a big blister in the middle of the prairie in the distant geological past. Erosion has carved it into a remarkable series of ridges and hills within the hills. To the north, gold was exposed by this erosion process and its discovery created a gold rush in the 1870s. That resulted in the near extermination of the Sioux Indians. These were their Sacred Mountains that we had, by treaty, recognized and promised to exclude from the White Eyes westward migrations and settlements. But the discovery of gold was a tidal wave that no government could restrain and the betrayal of the Native Americans would lead to the Little Big Horn slaughter in Montana and the massacre at Wounded Knee.

The jet plane headed out of the mountains toward the open plains and, I almost expected to see Kevin Kostner below chasing the buffalo and dancing with a wolf. There are a few thousand buffalo in the Custer State Park below, a small remnant of the millions that used to roam the plains before the advent of the White Eyes. The plane's wing dipped sharply, took a wide swinging maneuver, then began losing altitude quickly as it headed north for a stop at the Rapid City Airport. The airport was built only a few years ago outside of Rapid City on the wide open plains. I had never been to it, and I had never flown over this section of South Dakota.

"We'll have a stop of a half hour," the pilot announced. "Take your boarding pass with you if you go into the terminal."

I looked out the window again. The plains below were just that—plain and flat—as expected. The scene from the plane, however, was one I had never experienced before. The utter flatness of the plains was a extreme contrast to the verdant Black Hills that we had flown over only a few minutes ago. The scene was awesome.

The trip across time

The terminal at Rapid City didn't interest me. It was too new and sterile. No hustle and bustle of activity such as a bus terminal used to be. When I was younger, bus terminals fascinated me. They were a place to go to travel or just visit. In a bus terminal you could find the best cross-section of society you could ever hope to find. But air terminals. They were different. Everyone appeared too well off, too affluent. You needed money to travel by air. Bus terminals were available to everyone and every class and economic status used them. Most of them were gone now; shut down. Buses were becoming a thing of the past. Society would miss them.

I had left Sioux Falls in 1958, the day after I married Peggy Jones. Peggy was born in Sioux Falls and lived across from Longfellow Grade School. She went to school there with my brother, Jimmy. After graduating from WHS, she went to Chicago to work for a publishing house, but she returned to Sioux Falls in two years to attend Augustana College. While attending Augie, she was also secretary to Coach Bob Burns in the athletic department. We hit it off and were married in 1958. The day after our wedding, with all of our worldly goods in the trunk of our 1951 Buick, we left Sioux Falls for Colorado University where I would enroll in graduate school. The midwest was in a recession, but California was in the opposite situation. Jobs abounded and recruiters from California were offering jobs to those who would travel to the state. Two years later we were in California and I was teaching science in a high school.

I stayed in my seat. A half hour wait could end up being an hour wait sometimes—or longer. My mind started drifting back to the neighborhood I grew up in. Galesburg it was called. Actually the Gales Addition but everyone called it Galesburg. I was going back for a neighborhood reunion. My first. Everyone assured me that it was to be a day full of great fun and excitement. I pulled out and looked again at the postcard that had been sent to me in California by Bob Harvey.

This reunion had begun on a modest scale when a dying Galesburgite, Hank Davis, wanted to get together for one last time with his buddies. This great idea and first reunion became a tradition and it continued long after Hank passed away. Bob Harvey of the 'Sixth Avenue Gang' was eager for these reunions to continue, and he had taken it upon himself to contact anybody and everybody who had lived in the Galesburg area to let them know the date of the reunion at the American Legion. The Skadsons, Engles, Schmidts, Mongers, Sachens, Lehmans, Tunges, Stantons, Mofles, Ziskes, Roses, etc., etc, etc., would be there, he assured me when I had last seen him. It had been forty to fifty years since I had heard these names and I had forgotten so many of the faces that went with them. "Don't worry," Harvey had told me, "the names and faces will come back to you." I was really getting excited now thinking about the reunion. For me this would be an exhilarating experience to meet once again all of my old buddies. This once a year get-together always attracted a number of persons, like me, who had moved away. Many had become well established and very successful in their chosen communities after they found their way in the big world outside of the less affluent Galesburg of the 30s and 40s.

"Oh, by the way, Fred, the feed is free, but we do have one thing we like to do if you have any extra change. We collect money for various charity causes, to help boys mainly. It's something we started years ago for underprivileged kids that we wanted to help out. This time the Galesburg Gang will send boys to summer camp. As many as the group can afford. A few bucks from each person can add up to quite a sum."

I knew what it meant to be poor. My dad worked at the Sioux Falls Paint and Glass Company. He had worked up from ten cents an hour to almost fifty cents an hour pay, but this increase was still not enough for a family of ten. Eight kids in the family left little money for any one kid. Hand-me-down clothes were the rule. One pair of shoes a year for a growing boy was almost impossible to survive with. We went bare-footed most of the summer. I had dreamed at one time or another that I could go to a camp during the summer. It never happened, however, dream as I would. There just never was enough money available for us. The underprivileged 'Brooklyn' kids of Sioux Falls' had a hard struggle. But in spite of our seemingly underprivileged conditions and status in the community, I felt I had succeeded and it would feel good to help someone else growing up as most all of us could afford the little extra money now. Now I would do it for a unfortunate kid. A good idea, Bob!

Galesburg

As the Sioux River flows south meandering its way to its rendezvous with the Missouri River, it becomes temporarily sidetracked in an area where the Mesozoic Quartzite rock is exposed in southern South Dakota. The resistance of the land causes the Sioux to detour into an almost full circle so that its southern flowing waters flow east and then north again before being detoured again to the east and finally south toward the mighty Missouri. Over the millennia, this quirky oxbow configuration slowed the water down enough to make its turn and in the process deposited alluvium that made the ground flat and fertile in this broad valley. The higher ground in the center of the oxbow became a bulwark of resistance and stands like a medieval castle guarding the surrounding area that the river flows around. This commanding position overlooking the water offered a refuge from the rampages of the Sioux River after initial settlement on the lower flood plain was accomplished in the mid-l800s by the Dakota Land Company and the Western Town Company. Their development near the exposed quartzite falls was short-lived as Dr. J. L.. Phillips bought, laid claim to and platted the quarter section of the former army barracks area and carved out the outline for future development of the downtown business area. In the late l860s a town was beginning to manifest itself as stores, land offices and living quarters were developed.

To the south of J. L.. Phillips claim, four hundred acres of land were claimed by the successful realtor and merchant from St. Paul, Artemas Gale. This gently rolling land, bounded on the north by Twelfth Street, ran to the southern boundary of Eighteenth Street, then from Minnesota Avenue eastward to approximately Seventh Avenue. Dirt-lined Phillips Avenue rose a gentle grade from the downtown center where William Van Eps had erected his combination store and home and where Harry Corson was to build a hotel at Ninth and Phillips. Mr. Gale proceeded to build a home a respectable walking distance from the bustling downtown at about Fourteenth and Phillips after he platted the property for home sites and called it 'Gales Addition'. It became known as 'Galesburg'.

....

I began researching my family tree a few years ago. There's a branch of the United States Federal Archives—Ryan Archives—near my home in San Bruno, California, so I developed a habit of visiting it for an hour or two after work in the afternoon. I went crazy looking through the microfilms of the early census. They were fascinating. I took notes and then began writing little stories about the people I knew, both in Sioux Falls and in California. I began to think about everybody and everywhere as 'history'. But there was so much I did not remember at first, so I wrote letters and researched from books. I did whatever I could to fill in the gaps. Beginning with a few essays, I developed collections that were complete enough for a book. Names, events, what people I had known during my life in the Heartland were doing now intrigued me. I wanted to re-visit my past.

It would be great, I thought, to have a high-school or college reunion in Sioux Falls. Maybe I could spend some time there and put my vignettes into a book. First I would need to re-explore Sioux Falls, revisit my old haunts, and polish the mirror of memory to see what might be reflected.

I continued to wait for the plane to take off for Sioux Falls, but I grew sleepy. My mind drifted again. Thoughts about the first time I hitch-hiked to Wyoming started coming back. The trip through the Black Hills, standing by the roadside in Wyoming waiting for a ride....bits and pieces.

Hitch-hiking to see Uncle Bill in Wyoming

Uncle Bill moved from South Dakota to Sheridan, Wyoming, in the late '40s. Bill's appearance always reminded me of a Walt Disney cartoon character that I had seen in one of his western classics. He wore a black ten-gallon hat that dwarfed his five-gallon size. Added to his half-shaven appearance was a home-made cigarette dangling from the side of his mouth. His small metal-rimmed glasses framed wide-open, innocent-looking eyes, masking his devil-ish plots. He was always thinking of a way to embarrass you until you almost cried. Especially the girls. His cowboy boots were worn outside of his Levi's that hung loose on his slight frame. All of his brothers towered over him. Maybe that was the reason for his cocky attitude: defense.

Uncle Bill was a rare breed of individual that comes along once in a blue moon. He had a unique outlook on life. His actions, his humor, his easy-going friendly spirit, all packed into a slight five-foot two or three inches, made him standout as a 'one-of-a-kind' person. His sense of humor bordered on genius. If he had a Hollywood agent, he probably could have become the second Will Rogers of the Heartland. But then we could not have enjoyed his mischievous antics first hand, so it was just as well for us that he went undiscovered.

Bill had been a garbage collector in Sioux Falls, or in modern phraseology, a sanitary engineer. He lived with his wife, Alt, and daughter, Opal, on the east edge of the city on Southeastern Avenue, not too far from the Cherry Rock Bridge and vegetable gardens. (A condo was erected on the site in the 1990s.) His partners were the Van Diepen boys from the Riverside area. They would start work early in the morning, four or five o'clock, driving their hard-rubber-tired Franklin truck to collect refuse from all over the city. Their route was made up of scattered households as the city had no organized garbage collection system. Hauling trash and garbage was left to free enterprise and the hustle of individuals such as Bill, much as they still do today. This was the type of job Bill liked and excelled at. He liked moving around the city, seeing people, and was at ease with all types of personalities.

I had decided to hitchhike to see Bill in Sheridan, Wyoming. This was after working at a summer job at Girton Adams Ice Company. I actually had been fired from the job after my boss found out I was only fifteen years old. I was five-foot nine inches tall, weighed about one hundred eighty pounds and had successfully passed myself off as an eighteen-year-old. I could lift fifty, and hundred pound blocks of ice easily. One day the boss at Girton Adams approached me and told me he had to fire me because I was underage. "Come back when you're eighteen," he had said as he handed me my last paycheck. Now, I thought, would be a good time to go see Uncle Bill, my sister Nancy and my relatives who were raising her. Although hitchhikers were always looked upon with suspicion, it was still a good cheap way to travel. Also the potential for a great adventure made me want to try this trip.

The second 'hitch' was great. It was a salesman driver from Sioux Falls. This ride resulted in a lifelong friendship. The salesman bought me lunch and we had a good conversation from Chamberlain where he picked me up. The ride lasted all the way into Rapid City. The first night I spent at the Harney Hotel in a fifty-cent bed in the basement. Finding a hotel accommodation and sleeping in a hotel was a brand new experience for me. Next morning I was back on the road. After a half-hour of frustration, I started realizing that it was going to be a more difficult job hitchhiking through the Black Hills. A few three and four-mile rides finally got me past Mt. Rushmore and to Custer, but the rides were few and far between. Custer to Newcastle went fast with one good ride, then I had a long wait. The cars that came were few and far between, so I enjoyed the surrounding scenery. The next ride was strange. The older man didn't say much and drove looking straight ahead only with no conversation between us. Finally he apologized by saying this was as far as he could take me, and the pickup turned off a side road and stopped.

I got out.

Where the hell was I? In the middle of nowhere, I thought. I've been "nowhere" before. Nothing but a two-lane highway stretched out forever before me...

The roar of the massive jet engines suddenly woke me up. The summer trip to Uncle Bill's ranch was quickly pushed aside. Happily it ended up being the best summer I ever had. Bits and pieces. The plane lifted off from the Rapid City airport. What a marvelous feeling as the jet lifts off from the runway and you're airborne. My heart was wildly beating and I felt good that I was back in South Dakota again. And this time I was flying for the first time over the western part of the state. I had to take a deep breath and let it out slowly. The ground below was burnt brown, but a spectacular view of the Black Hills to the west presented itself. The plane banked to the right, dipped its wing low, and headed toward the east. In my hands was a map of South Dakota. I usually carry one while traveling on airplanes. To me, flying is the ultimate way to travel. Traveling at 35,000 feet at over five-hundred miles per hour while eating a sandwich has to be the traveler's dream. The map I carried helped me keep in touch with the reality of the earth. I spent a lot of time keeping track of where the plane was by searching for highways, rivers, hills, and mountains. I immediately found I-90 and then to the south of the Badlands, the White River. The White River's meandering pattern all the way to the Missouri River two-hundred miles away indicated its youth and lack of abundant water. It begins its wanderings to the Missouri River in the sand hills of Nebraska and drains some of the driest areas of western South Dakota. To the north of it, above the Pine Ridge Indian reservation, some of the most extensive Pleistocene fossils of mammals are exposed along the water-dissected Bad Lands National Park.

Twenty-five million years ago the entire area was bathed in water, creating marshes and swamps that nurtured with life. Around eighty-million years ago, the area was an ocean that teemed with sharks within and flying reptiles above. This waterway connected the Gulf of Mexico with the Gulf of Alaska, and it was responsible for the sandstone that became the quartzite deposition in the eastern part of the state. Dinosaurs roamed the land and ichthyosaurs (water dinosaurs) swam in the warm ocean. Extensive deposits of limestone in Kansas have sheltered fossils from the Cretaceous epoch of the United States. The land masses of North America have since then moved north and west, broken away from Africa and, in the process, created the Atlantic Ocean and the Rocky Mountains as well as the Black Hills. What a change has occurred. More recently, toward the end of the last Ice Age, huge woolly mammoths roamed the area along with the buffalo and early man. The early human inhabitants of the plains depended on both for their food supply. Only recently in Hot Springs a cache of mammoth fossils was discovered, shedding light on the past around the Black Hills. History. *A big bit. A big piece of the puzzle.*

The swamps are gone and it almost defies your imagination to visualize these past events as you look down from the airplane to the arid land below. This dry, hot area, however, presented an opportunity to Ted and Bill Hustead of Wall Drug. In hopes of luring tourists to their business, they offered free ice water to the parched and/or curious traveler. It worked. Wall Drug became history, and today it's known world-wide. While hitch-hiking to visit my Uncle Bill in Sheridan, Wyoming, I stopped for a free glass of water in 1948. The following year, Bill was in Montana, and I had caught a ride all the way from Chamberlain to Rapid City, so I didn't stop in Wall.

The plane trip to Sioux Falls from Rapid City is a short one. Only an hour of flying—barely enough time to reflect on all of the things that raced through my head. Right now, seeing this area for the first time from the air, really fascinated me. It also brought back the memory of my trip in 1947 along Highway 38 on my Whizzer motor bike. I was going to Mount Rushmore but the trip was cut short when my motor-bike quit running on me. That was another one of my adventures that I'll always remember with fond memories. Bits and pieces.

My mother passed away in August, 1944. I was 11 years old and in seventh grade. Her death almost tore the family apart. My father was always working, my mother was gone. Life was vacant. My sister, Dorothy, although only nineteen, began taking care of me and my brothers and sisters after there was talk putting me into the Children's Home on Tenth Street.

School at Longfellow started in September. My buddy, Ted, was setting pins at the Sport Bowl bowling alley and he talked me into working there also. In October I started setting pins at the downtown Sport Bowl. There were 16 alleys on its two floors and pinsetters were always in demand. It was hard physical work to set the ten pins up by hand (there were no automatic pin setting devices in 1944). It was a great challenge, a challenge to develop my body and t keep my mind focused on the job at hand. I loved it. And I could make some money.

The Second World War was nearing its fourth year and the Army Air Base in Sioux Falls was in full operation. Thousands of soldiers were being trained at the Air Base in radio techniques. All work and no play...in their off hours they sought entertainment. The Sport Bowl downtown, next to the Hollywood Theater on Phillips Avenue, offered bowling as well as arcade entertainment. The arcade part of the entertainment included pin ball machines, scooter ball, skill games, and the usual 'coney island' entertainment as well as a novelty shop that sold souvenirs for the folks back home. A small cafe was available to get food and socialize over cups of coffee. The Sport Bowl was where all of the action was, and it was a good place to meet girls. Some folks did not consider this a proper place for the good girls of the community to be seen in, however. It attracted what many thought to be the questionable young thrill seekers out for a lark. Whatever the view point, much of the soldiers' spare time was spent in the Sport Bowl. It was a very popular place.

The war was over in 1945, but the supply of automobiles and other mechanized vehicles had not caught up with the demand of the consuming public. I wanted some means of transportation to get around as I was tired of having to walk everywhere. My job at the Sport Bowl gave me more money than I had ever had. Some was used for spending money—for food, my own clothes that I bought now, and school paper—and I was able to save some of it. Thanks to Mr. Hilker, the manager of the Sport Bowl, who had set up an account of one-dollar in a local savings bank for a Christmas present, I had been introduced to systematically saving money. I was the first person in my immediate family who had ever started an account in a bank, thanks to the generosity of Mr. Hilker. This small gesture of one-dollar was to greatly influence my saving and spending practices for the rest of my life. I learned to be very conservative with money and, before long, I had saved $150. One hundred-and fifty-dollars. It seemed like a million dollars to a thirteen-year old.

Now that I had money, I could solve my transportation problems. But a car would cost too much. Gas, tires, license...too much money. After much thought about the type of transportation needed, I decided that I could afford something cheaper—a Whizzer Motor Bike. I had seen a few of these bicycles and the ease of handling and convenience impressed me. Storm's Bicycles, next to Metz Baking Company on the East Side, sold these bikes. After numerous visits to check them out, I finally decided to buy one.

The Whizzer gave me an exhilarating sense of freedom that I had never dreamed possible. I was able to expand my world immensely by exploring the Heartland to the fullest.

....

The population of South Dakota hovers around 700,000, maybe 800,000 souls, an extremely low density by most states' standards. Most of these are clustered in the Sioux Falls and Rapid City areas. That leaves a very low density for the rest of the state, and that is how they would like to keep it. The Missouri River bisects the state into the West River section and the East River section. They could not be more different. The West River mainly supports ranching with an 'Old West' style of living. The East River section has more moisture, and this encouraged the settling by many more farmers and merchants. The patchwork quilt design of the farms is the result of the surveyor's system of organizing the land into square miles patterns.

Towns fly by so quickly—or rather we do—as we pass from Chamberlain onward to the east until the largest city in South Dakota comes into view, Sioux Falls. The Sioux River almost surrounds the city, (in an oxbow pattern) creating the beautiful, peaceful Sioux Valley After almost encircling the city, it flows to the east and finally to the south to enter the Missouri River in Sioux City. The river was the single greatest factor that motivated the early settlers to settle on this piece of the prairie.

As the plane makes its slow descent, the quartzite quarries can be seen west of the airport in West Sioux. The Interstate lies just to the west of them now. I catch sight of the pioneer monument on the high point north of town on a bluff overlooking the Sioux Valley. Suddenly, with a jolt, the airplane settles down on the runway. I'm home.

The memories flood my mind and the past rushes in like a tidal wave, carrying me through the airport in a daze.

The Sioux Falls Paint and Glass was at the busy corner of Ninth Street and First Avenue until it was razed in 1974. My father got a job there during the depression and worked for over thirty years as a glazer.

PHILLIPS AV N—Contd
Lacotah Bldg—Contd
14△Bradfelt Collection
△Bradfelt Finance Co
△Medical Dental Service Bureau
15 Vacant
16△Gusarson Carl E
17△Fylken Ann chiro
18 Monarch Sales Co adv
19-20△Sioux Motor Clnr Co
Street continued
123△Leather Shop The
△Luggage Shop The
△Hyde Hadleigh D optometrist
△Hyde Hadleigh D jr optometrist
124△Kaybee Store
125△Hyde Frank Jewelry Co
△Hyde Frank Realty Co
125½△Gore Jack 11
126△Leader The women's clo
127 Vacant
128△Coney Island Lunch
128½ Peterson Edith Mrs 4
129-31△S & L Co (dept store)
130△Ace Wall Paper & Paint Stores
△Mulhair Robt J pntr contr
132△E & W Clothing Co Inc
133△Coleman The Florist
133 VanEps (1886) Block
Rooms:
200△Hanson Realty & Loan Co
202△Grant Harry A lawyer
204△Trad Studio photog
205 Vacant
206 Vacant
207△Scott Engineering Co Inc
208-09△Rohde E W Bkpg Service
210△Minnehaha County Tuberculosis Assn
212△Woodmen Accident Ins Co
215△Smith Jesse G phys
△VanLier Pieter C phys
217 Vacant
300△Waul Jas P 1
301 Christensen Janet 1
302 Welch Frank 1
304△Gotthelf Joe 2
306 Parsley Geo 1
307△Elofson Eliz H Mrs 1
308 Edgerly Clinton L 3
309 Wiedenhoeff Adolph 1
310 Vacant
311 Lutterman David 1
312 Jacobson Jacob A 1
315 Lindblad Anton E 2
316 Mellquist Fred S 2
317 Diedrich John 1
318 Koppe Augustina 1
Street continued
134△Granada Theatre
135△Federated Finance Co
bsmt Windsor Barber Shop
136△Tick-Tock Cafe

136 Strand Building
bsmt Vacant
Rooms:
200△Lee Loan Co
201△Simmons Corwin J dentist
204△Halvorson Lawrence R real est
205-07△Rapid Emp Service
206△Springfield Group of Fire Ins Co's
209-11 Vacant
210 Vacant
212 Vacant
215△US Rent Control Office
△US Census Bureau
8th intersects
200△Nickel Plate System No 4 and ofc
201△Dunning Drug Store
202△Rainbow Bar
△Bohl Julia Mrs 3
203△Midcontinent Broadcasting Co Inc
△Stanley Home Products
△KELO Radio Station
204△American Dist Tel Co
△Western Union Tel Co
205△Davis Bros Inc tires
206△Terry Wm M clnr
206½△Henning Edw O 2
207△Paramount Bar
207½△Robertson Wm 7
209△Coast to Coast Store auto access
210△K & K Co (dept store)
211△Fahrendorf Lester M chiro
212 Hollywood Theatre
bsmt△Art Kraft Commercial Display
213△Harry's Pool Hall
213½△Grand Hotel
Pine Gladys Mrs 7
214-18△Family Drug & Beverage Store
215△Cut Rate Army Store
△O K Barber Shop
Heinje Leona beauty shop
217△Electric Supply Co Inc
219△Blue Front Cleaners
220△Holly Cafe
221△Merit Stores No 3
Merit Stores Fixit Shop
Barry Kenneth radio repr
221½ Perry Block
Rooms:
1△Frommes' beauty shop
2△Gartland Robt J dentist
3△Knutson John O Co mdse brokers
4 Dirksen Kath 1
5 Speulda Ralph E 1
6△Hawkeye Casualty Co
7 Woods Fern E 1
8 Alguire Shirley 1
9△Edwards Emily Mrs 2
Street continued
222△Sport Bowl Inc bowling
△Pelley J Osee restr
△Sport Bowl Novelty Shop

11

By 1965, Sioux Falls was on the verge of a redevelopment project that would change the 'old' downtown. The Sioux Falls Paint and Glass at the foot of Ninth Street and First Avenue, where my father worked for over thirty years, would be razed as well

Sioux Falls
1965

as *Fenn's Ice Cream and Parker Storage on First Avenue. Many businesses along tenth street, east from Phillips Avenue to the river, would suffer from the bulldozer. The creation of Faywick Park would soften the blow of this once industrial area.*

4

PHILLIPS AV S—From 9th south beyond city limits, dividing line for streets running east and west
100△Ronning Pharmacy
Emerson Block
Rooms:
 1 Hagen Martha Mrs 1
 2 Gustafson John 2
 3 Vacant
 4 Narveson Gusta 1
 5 Combs Price 2
 6 Aasen Oscar 2
 7-8 Morris Hoye L 5
 9 Vacant
10△Hakl Lillian C 1
11△Garrison Beauty Shop
20-21△Pitchford Mabel Mrs 3
22 Fields Wm 1
23 Skrovig Thora 1
24△Williams Leah Mrs 1
25 Flater Margt Mrs drsmkr
26 Vandanacker Kathleen
27 Beck Marie 1
28 McClellan Eliz Mrs 1
29 Fritz Jacob 1
30 Eidness Gus 1
Street continued
101△Barkalow Bros Co cigars
102△Nickel-Plate System No 3 restr
103△Roth's men's clo
104△Coyote Bar liquor
105△Schiffs Shoes
106△Chocolate Shop
108△Olson E C Co men's clo
110 **First National Bank Bldg**
 △First Natl Bank & Trust Co
Rooms:
200-01△Stanton H A Inc ins
202△Cherry, Brithwaite & Cadwell lawyers
212△Sanford Realty Co
216-18△Necomb J P Finance Co
219 Jay Ralph A tailor
221 Vacant
222 Vacant
223 Vacant
224 Vacant
225 Vacant
226-27 Vacant
300-01△S D State Medical Assn
 S D Journal of Medicine & Pharmacy
 △S D Board of Medical & Osteopathic Examiners
302 Vacant
303-04 Bender Albert G 2 jan
Street continued
111△Montgomery Ward & Co (dept store)
116△Farmers Market furn
117△Penney J C Co (dept store)
120△Horwitz Jewelers

120½ **Beach-Pay Building**
Rooms:
 1△Walters Chas E dentist
 2△Public Finance Co
 6△Hanson Studio photogs
 7△Gage Edw E 4
 9△Valansky Helen D chiropodist
3d fl Woodman Hall
 Coris Danl 1
 △Ganas Robt J 1
 Brown Jas 1
 △Ray Gust 1
Street continued
121△Kinney G R Co shoes
121½△Han-De Work Mart
 △Campbell Ethelind 1
122△Pay's Art Store
123-27△Woolworth F W Co (5c and 10c store)
124△Linpark Clothes
124½ **Pay Block**
 △Heinz Edw B dentist
 △Kerwood Lillienne Mrs 1
 △Cox Arnold E 1
 △Miller's Beauty Salon
126△Johnson Shoe Co
126½△Central Hall
 Norse Glee Club
 Sons of Norway
 Degree of Honor
 Royal Neighbors of Am
 Church of Jesus Christ of Latter Day Saints
128△Weatherwax F H Co clo
128½△Beightol Florabelle Mrs beauty shop
 △Gruetzmann Charlotte L A Mrs drsmkr
 △Green Dragon Studios photogs
129△Baker's Shoe Store
131-35△Newberry J J Co (5c and $1.00 store)
132△Time Theatre
132½ **Times Theatre Bldg**
 △Goque Mabel C drsmkr
 △Peterson Ella H Mrs 1 drsmkr
 △Olson Martin A chiro
136△Hecker's Men's Store
 E 10th intersects
200△Kopel's women's apparel
201△Kresge S S Co (5c to $25c store)
204△Sunshine Food Markets
205½ **Kresge Building**
Rooms:
200△Western Finance Co
202△Hanson Carl E dentist
204△Lanam Merwin O phys
206△Mortrude Melvin O deutist
 △Nelson Melvin O dentist
208-09△State Farm Ins Co
210-11△Whitcher Dale D dentist
212△Logeman Daisy Mrs buttons
214△Hanson A Talman optometrist
216-17△Hegg-Armstrong Co real est
220△B B Letter Shop

14

10TH E—Contd
111△Davis Tailors
111½△Hamburger Inn
112△Dakota Lndry & Dry Clnrs (br)
 △Greenfield LeRoy H barber
bsmt Davis Tailors (shop)
113△Delmont Bar
113½△Big Three Garage
114-34△Fenn Bros Inc ice cream
 mfrs
115△Rushmore Cafe restr
117△Idle Hour Recreation Parlor ⋈
 S 1st av intersects
 CRI&PRy crosses
204△Otis Elevator Co
 △Munce Bros Trans & Stge
 △Linde Air Products
 △Mid-Continent Refrigerator Co
 Paxton-Gallagher
 Peet H E Paint Co
 Lorillard P Co tobacco
 △Evans J D Equipment Co road
 equip
210△Lorin Packard Co autos
212△Brown Drug Co whol druggists
218△Tri-State Tobacco & Candy Co
220△Clements Auto Co (repr dept)
 6
 S 2d av intersects
300△Rushmore Service Station
302△Pantry Lunch
 Sioux River
 12
 S Reid ends
401△Jordan Millwork Co (mill)
421△Zabel Louis (whse)
428 Zabel Louis (whse)
 CMStP&PRy underpass
 GNRy underpass
 CStPM&ORy underpass
 S Franklin av intersects
701 Wood Howard Stadium
800△Schaefer Bldg Mterils
802△Lien Leonard R filling sta
806 Eight-O-Six Club
 S Indiana av intersects
808△Corn States Serum Co
 Simons LeRoy 6
808½ Flora Loren 3
 S Fairfax av intersects
1000△Kinsley Wayne H 5
1002 Koepp Albert C 3
1004△Brown Roy J 3 ◎
1006△Fisher Augusta A Mrs 1 ◎
1008△Posthuma John 2 ◎
1012△Davidson Ida Mrs 5
1016△Witt Earl H 6
1016½ Dailey Erma Mrs 2
1018△Anderson Walfred E 5 ◎
 S French av intersects
1100△Buck John O 2 ◎
1104 In'tVeld Adrian 3
1106 Vacant
1108△Skrondahl Louie J 4 —
1110△Boelter Ervin M 5

1126△Embassy Club
 S Cliff av intersects
1200△Lyle & Albert's Service
1202△Middlen Wm J beer
1212△Edwards Russell 4 ◎
1218△Jones Amos 2 ◎
1102△Buck John O vet
1220△Hooker Jas R 5 ◎
1227△Garness Elmer C 6
 S Sherman av intersects
1301△S D Children's Home Society
 △Garness Elmer C supt
1310 Hall Richd S 2
 S VanEps av intersects
1400 Wheelock Louis E 2 ◎
1401△Letrud Edw G 2
1402△Coome John R 2
1403 Hanger Christine Mrs
 △Young Eldon D 2
1404△Earle Chas E 3
1405△Rehschuch Geo 3 ◎
1409△White Maurice W 2
1409½ Donahue Leroy 2
1411△Power Wm C 2
 S Wayland av intersects
1501△Grask Trailer Sales
1504△Romslo Allan C 3 ◎
1506△General Builders Supply Co
1508△Sioux Amusement Co
1510△Assam Hamad gro
1513△North Technical Institute
1515△North Technical Institute
 Health Center
 △N T I Grill restr
1517 Vacant
1517½△Lee's Lila Progressive School
 of Dancing
 △Thoms Leonard W 4
 S Blauvelt av intersects
1601 Keyman Henry 4
1603△Knutson Chas A 2 ◎ watch repr
1605 Keyman Jas W 4
1606△Binker Otta A 2 ◎
1607△Smith John F 2 ◎
1609 May Henry jr 5 ◎
1618△Krohn Albert J 4 ◎
 S Mable av intersects
1701△Stephenson Ralph T 2 ◎
1703△Crowe Elmer 5 ◎
1705 Gillett Lyle 2 ◎
1707△Rudolph Jas W 3 ◎
1709△Haugse Ole H 4
1711△Sather Henry O 5 ◎
1805 Wareham Geo barber
 △Lodermeier Eug J 5 ◎
 SF Taxidermy Shop
1809△Boyd Lyle R gro
1825△Dr Pepper Bottling Co
 Mission Orange Btlg Co
 S Highland av intersects
 S Jessica av intersects
1903△Midwest Oil Co filling sta
 Ace Auto Court
1931△Helgerson David 5 ◎ filling sta
 S Lewis av begins
 S Chicago av begins
2101△Monger Hildur auto repr
2107△Vincent Edw ◎ beer

1950

The Pride of Sioux Falls and the Heartland

Bud Adams • Pauline Adams Hanson • Nettie Adler • Ellen Mae Aggergaard • Ronald Ahrendt • Marlys Ahrendt • Anna Mae Rose Marie Albert • Donna Mae Allen • Barbara Amland • Dee Brewer Amos • Bonnie Anderson • Courtney Anderson • Ken Anderson • Bob Anderson • Don Anderson • Mervin Andersen • Ron Anderson • Russell Anderson • Wallace Anderson • Kenneth Anderson • Robert Anderson • Roger Anderson • W. C. Anderson • Pat Paul Donna Kirkeby Earl Angle Grayce Willadsen Roessler Angle • Lois Antrim • Milt Archer • Ruth Harold Arnott • Laura Assid • Betty Seeley Atkins • Alvin Auch • Sandy Bingham Aults • Corlus Austin • Marilynne Bachman • Dean Baker • Delores Baker • Joyce Baker • Burl Baker • W. S. Baker • Roger Joan Erickson Bakke • Vernon Barck • Lorraine Barnes • Donald Bartholow • Dennis Bartling • Mitzi Baustuan • Clara Beam • Ronald Beatty • Bonnie Beck • Bob Dick Ron Beck • Duane Beckstrom • Wanita Behymer • James Bell • Joanne Bell • Oretta Bender • Coletta Benning • Orlander Benson • Bob Berdahl • Carol Berg • Priscilla Berthelsen • Gwen Bertelsen • John Berven • Ted Donna Marv Kevin Francis Brad Brian Gary Beuckens • Jane Keegan Bills • Marie Wilcox Bingen • Lillian Bingham • Robert Bittner • Charlotte Blackman Seubert • Gloria Gulbrandson Block • Joyce Bloem • Robert Blue • Ray Bly • Rodney Boade • Diana Boe • Dick Boettcher • Harry Bogdos • Gail Bottge • Connie Sikkink Bowen • Dick Bowen • Dale Bowen • Patricia Boyle • Donna Boysen • Florence Braa • Bill Bradley • Marge Caldwell Bradley • Renella Brande • Bernice Brandenburg • Harlen June Fredricks Linda Hebert Diane Moberly Wendell Kenneth Russell Jeffery Brandt • Linda Tracy Shawn Chad Miranda Cole Hebert Mark Diane Matthew Meghan Moberly Wendell Patricia Nathan Lindsey Brandt • Kenneth Gayle Sebbo Jamie Jessica Christopher Martha Warsing Jenny David Jessica Brandt • Russell Candy Wahl Brandt • Jeffrey Margareta Niome Brandt • Dina Brandt • Harriet Branson • Dorothy Brasel • Joanne Brasel •

continued on page 57

16

2
Return after Thirty Years

The sky was clear, the sun bright and warm. I had returned to Sioux Falls. I had come home. But was it home? Can you really go home again? I was met at the airport by my sister, June Brandt. We drove to Russell Street and headed for our sister Dorothy's place in West Sioux, passing the new sports complex—the Howard Wood football/track stadium and convention center. I remembered the new stadium had been used the year after I graduated from Augie (1957). My sister, Dorothy, and her husband, Vern Daggett, had bought a house in West Sioux in the early 1950s while I was living alone in a house on Madison Street.

It was great to be back in her house drinking coffee, eating home-made cinnamon rolls, and having at good conversation. Dorothy always has a pot of coffee on the stove and she is great at making everyone feel welcome. Her house continually attracts a diverse group of visitors.

I was anxious to see the town, so I borrowed June's car. I was to be home for only a short time and I was anxious to revisit old haunts and see if I could find any of my old acquaintances. Already I had become familiar with the newer road system, the Interstate—I-90. It was very visible from the air as I had crossed South Dakota. The narrow, dangerous two-lane highways #16, #38 and #77 of the '50s had been replaced by the separated, one-directional two lane Interstate in the 1970s.

In 1940 the population of Sioux Falls was over 40,000 people. The 1950 population had grown to over 52,000 and by 1960 it was over 65,000. Now Sioux Falls and the surrounding areas boast over a quarter of a million people. A lot of things had been happening to accommodate this huge influx of people.

In the 1950s the city was bursting at the seams, but the pressure had been alleviated somewhat by the development of new housing starting in the eastern farm fields. The Korean War was still on in Asia and I had been drafted into the Army. I was in Europe serving my country at the time of the initial construction of these houses. Sioux Falls apparently could move forward without my presence.

This new growth in the Sioux Valley necessitated the development of services that were closer and more convenient to the housing. No longer did the people want to commute through the congestion of the downtown for their supplies. The roads were congested, the parking was inadequate and aggravated by the advent of revenue-producing parking meters that went against the grain of the conservative customers. They welcomed any business that was nearer to their homes, and this decreased the profit of the long established businesses in the downtown area. There was talk of gutting the downtown with Federal redevelopment money, a carrot dangled before communities to stimulate and rejuvenate downtown buildings across the nation. With little fanfare, the winds of change were blowing and massive new construction projects and events were to become a factor that would change Sioux Falls forever.

By 1968 when the Western Mall was constructed at Forty-first Street and Western Avenue, a group of business men found Sioux Falls to be fertile ground for new marketing ideas. Customer parking convenience, for example, and a new concept of national franchising (McDonalds, Wendys, Home Depot, Barnes and Nobel, etc., etc.) swept through the business world. Lost would be construction of buildings that had character and permanence, and in their place would be built super-efficient, bland, disposable structures. It was the beginning of businesses moving to the available open spaces in the southwestern area of Sioux Falls. The Western Mall was to be followed by the introduction of the Empire Mall in the 1970s. The time was ripe for small businesses to begin filling in the 'gaps' that were left on Forty-first Street and surrounding areas.

Streets had begun making a transition to handle the new patterns of traffic. Many streets such as Tenth and Minnesota Avenue were widened to help alleviate the car and truck traffic that was choking the main roads.

Another event that greatly influenced the trend of development in the Heartland was planned in the 1950s and initiated by the Federal Government in the 1960s. The Second World War had made one thing very clear about the transportation system in our large country—it was not very easy to travel rapidly or smoothly across the country. Germany had developed its rapid transit system, called the Autobahns, during the 30s and this aided them greatly in moving around their borders during the War. The United States had no such transportation system, but this was to be rectified beginning in the late 1950s. By the early 1960s a wide four-lane east-west Interstate System (I-90)was completed to the north of the city of Sioux Falls. Eventually a connecting north-south Interstate (I-29) was built that encompassed west side of Sioux Falls. An additional connecting link, I-229, bisected the southern and eastern open fields surrounding the city. These new, uncluttered lanes greatly reduced some of the congestion of the downtown streets, but it also opened up areas to development that had not been considered before—especially along Forty-first Street. A lot of businesses that were along the old established highways were impacted, some quit, but at the same time new modern businesses sprang up along the Interstate.

The old, rural, gravel-lined Forty-first Street would become a focal point along which Sioux Falls would attract most of its future prosperity.

Phillips Avenue Celebration

I headed downtown. I wanted to drive down Phillips Avenue, a street that I had "cruised" many a time in the 1940s and '50s, on foot and later in high school in my brother's 1935 Chevy. Phillips Avenue had been a magnet to me in my youth. Here was where the action was. The movie houses, the constant movement of autos up and down the street—these all were a part of my beginnings. Many times in the late evening I would leave my house where I lived alone in West Sioux and take a walk to the downtown. It had felt good walking along the now deserted streets by myself. It was a good time for thinking.

In 1951 when I first entered Augustana College, South Dakota State had beaten Augustana by a score of 58 to 7. In 1955 the score had been 28 to 0. State hadn't allowed Augie a touchdown in that hard fought game in '55. I didn't forget these games. I couldn't. They had been humiliating to me as a freshman and again as a junior at Augustana College. This year, as a senior, I was going to try and change the score. Augie had never beaten State at football, and I vowed that this was to be the year of change.

The following week the contest was to be held in Brookings against South Dakota State. State had been pegged for second place in the league, and the word was out that they were not going to roll over and lose like the University had.

From the start of the game, all of us Augie players played with a passion never before seen by the fans. We played over our heads and the State players were stunned. Augie was suppose to be a push-over. We were suppose to be the pits. A 'nothing' game for State. A scrimmage for State. Nothing but a warm up for the real game with the U, their coach had said. But we Augie players had other things in mind. From the very beginning of the game, Augie took command. Slant right, slant left, pass over the center to Walton...we kept hammering away. Slowly the State players retreated. A score for Augie on a pass from Nelson to Jones. Jones had a bloody face and a broken nose, but he still caught the ball for the score. Then Phil Nelson kicked the extra point. Seven to nothing—Augie ahead.

We had never played this tough before. The State players were sure Augie would cave in before the game was over. But it wasn't to be. We continued to outsmart, outplay, and outscore State. When the contest ended, Augie had beaten State by a score of 21 to 20. Again the margin of victory was Phil Nelson's extra points. No matter what the difference was, Augustana had beaten State as well as the University for the first time and in the same season!

The locker room after the game was a mad house. The players could hardly get into the locker room. Fans were everywhere congratulating the weary Augie players. Former Governor Joe Foss came into the locker room and congratulated the players. The mood of the players was one of shock. What had just happened here? Many sat on the benches not yet comprehending the victory completely. Although they had won, it still seemed totally unreal, like a dream.

On the return bus trip to Sioux Falls that night, on Highway 77, the players settled down to rest and quietly absorb the reality of their success. After leaving Brookings I sat back in my seat and relaxed. It had been a hard fought game and I was tired. After twenty minutes on the road, I got a very odd feeling. I had noticed that for a long time since leaving Brookings, there had been no cars passing the bus. The bus reached the half-way mark on the return trip and this same strange feeling crept over the other players and the coaches. What was wrong? I couldn't put my finger on it, but I knew something was going on that was unusual. All of the cars that had driven to the Brookings game had disappeared. All of a sudden it dawned on all of us that the cars from Sioux Falls were all behind the bus. Quick glances out of the back window confirmed this. A long line of headlights could be seen on the road. Miles and miles of cars were behind the bus. The people who had seen the game were giving the players a strange and wonderful ovation for our performance at Brookings. What a tribute to the conquering football team!

We reached the city limits of Sioux Falls. Normally the bus-load of players would return to the Augie campus after a game, but the coaches decided to change the routine. When the bus and the escorting cars approached downtown Sioux Falls, the bus driver was instructed to drive through the center of town, up Phillips Avenue and down Main, before returning to the Augie campus. What a spectacle the caravan created as it made its way through the city with horns blaring and lights blinking. Sioux Falls had not experienced the likes of this in a coons age. After two runs up and down the downtown streets, the bus returned to the Augie campus. A victory parade...and I was in it. Never in a thousand years, I thought. Phillips Avenue took on a different meaning for me after the Augustana victory parade that evening.

I had been warned by my sisters that there had been a lot of changes. I was not fully prepared for what I was about to see. The streets had been totally transformed. Gone were the Egyptian, Dakota and Granada Theaters where I had spent many hours of my youth pursuing my fantasies. Coney Island Lunch, S. S. Kresge, J. J. Newberry 5 & 10 cent store, J. C. Penneys, Wards, Cataract Hotel—almost everything I had known, gone. I felt betrayed. Cities were not suppose to change this fast. Not my town.

I went to the city library and the librarian directed me to some information about the happenings of Phillips Avenue and the area after I left Sioux Falls in 1958. What I found out almost made me cry. I also found out why I had left. Money. The Heartland had been in a mild recession in the 1950s, and I had been unfortunate enough to have finished college when there had been the lowest demand for my education. I couldn't find a job anywhere that would utilize my education degree. I found a part-time job at the post office that was in the old quartzite Federal Building at the intersection of Phillips and Twelfth. As a sub I could work unlimited hours, get in a lot of overtime, and make about $100 a week. Good money. However, in January of 1958, I was told that I must either become a regular postman or quit. Decision time was here. The regulars made about $60 to $70 a week. I didn't feel I could live on that. I now had a little money in my pocket, a newer car (1952 Buick, two-door black and red Special) and the need to settle down. I had been going with Peggy Jones since I graduated from Augie, and we had been talking about getting married. We decided to take the plunge. I bought a $20 gold ring in a moment of weakness and began contemplating our future. I worked right up to the day I left the post office. I quit, got married, left Sioux Falls and resumed my education at the University of Colorado in Boulder. I was now a married man.

Urban Renewal—1970s and 80s

"Major Downtown Renewal Work Began in 1970" read the headlines of the Sioux Falls Argus-Leader issue of Wednesday March 16, 1977. Marc Manderscheid, a junior at Augustana College, vividly recounts the sequence of Downtown Urban Renewal in Sioux Falls since its inception in May 1966. Spurred on by promise of Federal Government money to back the concept of 'newer is better', the established business community was to be shown the errors of their ways by committees of citizens who wanted to change the direction of the commercial development in the downtown. Of upmost importance was the need for parking. The prosperity of the 1940s resulted in a car buying revolution. Cars directed the consumers but the downtown was 'maxed out' for parking spaces then. These thoughts had actually been in many businessmen's minds long before the 1970s. It had been boom and bust for many of them for too many years. The recession of the 1950s was still fresh and many thought that the only solution to the downtown problem was to start anew. This was to be done by wholesale razing of old established buildings in order to open the area to new investment and tenants that would construct modern facilities for the downtown area.

Selected areas of downtown Sioux Falls were to be gutted. First off, the entire block between Seventh and Eighth Streets and Phillips to Main Avenue, the heart of the original downtown, would be razed. Seventh Street was to be eliminated along here. Then in 1970, the Downtown Holiday Inn, boasting a ten-story building with two restaurants, two bars, assembly rooms, and 208 guest rooms, was to be built. It opened in January 1972. In the meantime, a new six-story building to house Northwestern National Bank was built to the south of the Holiday Inn in the block between Eighth and Ninth Streets and Phillips and Main Avenues. The infamous Harbor Bar was torn down, along with the 'Francis rooms' that were above it. Many of the gentlemen and college students who frequented the rooms also had to "relocate".

The old quartzite-stone Carnegie Library on Tenth Street had become too small for the modern age. Pioneer grocery store, Look's Market, was razed and relocated. On December 26, 1972, a new library replaced the store on a half block to the west of the Holiday Inn. Moving south, the City Commission opened bids for a two-block Phillips Avenue mall that was eventually completed in November 1973. This mall effectively blocked car traffic from Phillips Avenue and opened it only to foot traffic. As the buildings downtown were razed, many of the merchants either closed or relocated to the south of town on the forty-first street shopping corridor. By the early 1990s this concept was not working and the downtown mall was ripped out and opened to car traffic again. The loss of customers was too great for the downtown merchants, many of whom were not around to see the mistake rectified.

In 1974 plans were made to acquire the properties on the east side of Phillips and north of the tallest structure in the block, the old National Bank of South Dakota Building. The old Granada Theater (in the Strand Building) was to be razed. The magnificent Egyptian Theater on Tenth Street had already been demolished, the Time Theater on Phillips between Hecker's and Weatherwax's Clothing stores was shut down. The Dakota Theater, home of the western movie, across from the Granada on Phillips became only a memory. At this point there were only two theaters operating in the downtown area: the Hollywood and the State Theaters. By the 1990s these too would be torn down or vacated.

The pleasure centers that had existed in the downtown area had been losing customers steadily since WW II. The new rage—drive-in theaters like the Starlite and East Side—allowed parents and kids to see outdoor movies in the privacy of their automobiles. Entire families could attend the movies at a very moderate price. Fewer people went to the downtown area to spend their money. The established theaters felt the effects of this change, but were still optimistic. The advent of television in the 1950s, however, became the theaters' death-knoll. TV was sweeping the country. It produced continuous home entertainment that didn't require dressing up or traveling downtown. When the Western Mall was opened a new concept of smaller, multiple theater under one roof dominated the movie theater thinking. The older theaters could not compete.

I drove by the old Washington High School building on Main Avenue. It is no longer a school building but nevertheless it is used for education. As the distance to the high school increased with each new house being constructed farther and farther away, expanding the circumference of the school district, and as new elementary schools were being built, the old centrally-located high school looked less and less viable. Like an old flame, she appealed less and less as she got older, until the old quartzite building finally was abandoned as an educational facility in 1992.

The break with the past is now complete.

In the fall of 1992, a new modern Washington High School rose up out of farm land east of Sioux Falls at Sixth and Sycamore. It was the culmination of many years of concern and planning by the school board to provide adequate space, modern facilities, and a more accessible school for the changing demographic character of the Sioux area which had reached a population of over 100,000. The old Highway 38 that took you from Sioux Falls to Valley Springs and beyond had been ripped out, and new streets were built to accommodate the housing explosion that had been going on in the area for many years.

In an expansion too far along to ignore now, the people of the city had been moving onto the once-fertile farmlands that surrounded Sioux Falls. Decisions had to be made by the School Board. In 1965 Lincoln High School was constructed, and this was the first overt attempt to keep up with the rapid changes of population in the Sioux Valley. The elementary schools were overcrowded. Washington High School was bursting at its seams with students. It had been a long time coming and it was completed none too soon for the thousands of future students that were to pass through its doors.

And a new use was proposed for the beautiful quartzite building. After much debate and research, the community decided to use Washington High as an exploratorium for the kids of the Heartland and an entertainment center for the adults who had, after all, paid for the building with their taxes and to whom it rightfully belongs. A new auditorium for the arts and a science center were to be built—the Washington Pavilion. The old building would be saved from the wrecking ball. That little flame in the old girl was not about to flicker out and die.

Forty-first Street—1990s

I decided that there was one more last area that I had to see before I quit for the day.

I drove south on Minnesota Avenue to Forty-first Street. I wanted to absorb all of the changes that had happened. I turned right on Minnesota and Forty-first—the corner of the old South Sioux Falls—and slowly headed west. I passed my nephew's shop—Bob's Lock and Key—but I decided I was too tired to stop now.

I recognized nothing else in the area.

23

I had been told that the six or eight-lane cement-paved thoroughfare was busy all of the daylight hours, a far cry from the situation a few years ago. Long traffic lines at the stop light are routine now. I observed that better signal-lights are needed in order to take left-hand turns. The double left-hand turn lane in the center of Forty-first's multi-lane street is too dangerous.

Getting onto the broad, busy thoroughfare was an even more challenging experience.

It was only a few years before in these open fields that the first airport had been built. The South Sioux Falls community was accustomed to being left alone to themselves. Now Forty-first street had been widened numerous times since the black-topped two-lane road was upgraded in the early 1970s. That was when the first explosion of business construction was occurring following the development of the Western Mall at the corner of Western and Forty-first Street in 1968. This and similar malls had followed the Park Ridge Mall in 1955 to respond to the changing needs of the new consumer class. A large multi-business complex with adequate hassle-free parking for untold numbers of cars was a revolution that began in the Heartland in the 50s. Although the traditional downtown buildings had character, the eighty-year-old cramped, cluttered and outdated downtown shopping area on Phillips and Main had not and could not respond to the explosive increase in the number of automobiles that raced off the assembly lines after W.W. II. The winds had been changing, but few established businessmen had understood which direction the breezes were blowing.

This situation changed radically in 1968 with the construction of the Western Mall. Acres of undeveloped river bank land were waiting to be developed. The river had been tamed, and it was time the land was put to use for the increased population that was burgeoning at the city limits of this midwestern city.

Floods were a minimal threat since the Corps of Engineers corrected Mother Nature's folly of running the seemingly uncontrollable Sioux River around the outskirts of this developing metropolis.

A river cutoff to the north helped correct this quirk of nature. Construction of a new channel to the north of the city that connected the open link in the large oxbow pattern of the river had been attempted many times in the past, but failed each time. However, new engineering techniques and tools sparked a renewed confidence for success at this time. The serpentine meandering of the Sioux River in West Sioux Falls was obliterated with dirt, replaced by a straight no-nonsense channel. No longer would the meandering river offer a lazy afternoon of fishing and swimming as it had done for many a young boy.

The lack of curves in the river's channels minimized the chance of flooding as had occurred in 1957. A new and controllable bank for the river was built throughout its western length. The terror of a downtown flood at its bend had been somewhat lessened when a quartzite wall was constructed, but the volume of water in the river which was a key to flood relief had never been controlled until the recent completion of the north bypass. This new approach would make the problem history. Something to read about in the history book. A thing of the past.

I reached the Interstate on-ramp. I took it. The day had been very stressful for me. I was tired, and I needed rest and a chance to digest what I had learned.

Food in the Heartland

June was waiting for me. It was supper time and she had made my favorite meal—meatloaf, mashed potatoes, lettuce salad, home-made rolls, and string beans. For dessert there was home-made cake. South Dakota food, not California food.

Few topics create such instant conversation as *food*. The midwest is a food conversation haven. Where else in the United States can you find so many good, wholesome, home-cooked type restaurants per square mile as in the Heartland cities? The food is always piled high on the plates, with apologies for it not being enough. It is filling, satisfying, nourishing, and abundant. And at the family smorgasbords, if you don't get enough the first time around, you're expected to take another helping. Places like Bonanza, the Cracked Pot, Brenners (Walt and Mary's), K. C. 's, Rosie's, and the dozens of other homey-named eating establishments, pride themselves on their large following of repeat customers. never turning away unsatisfied customers. And the prices are extremely reasonable for so much.

For those born in the 20s and 30s you were taught to eat everything that was put before you. You dutifully obeyed, be it beets, rutabagas, or broccoli. Some items may have taken longer to get from the plate to your mouth and at times you might almost have fallen asleep at the table resisting and procrastinating in hopes that Mom would forget that you were there, but the underlying lesson was learned—eat all of the food the Good Lord gave you. Nothing was to be wasted.

As youngsters this lesson was not very difficult to apply in our large family of eight kids. We had voracious appetites from our non-stop playing and we would eat almost anything. On our playing rounds of the neighborhood, carrots were pulled from gardens and eaten without benefit of being washed because that took time. Apple trees didn't have their apples on them for long, and handouts of food were always looked for and welcomed. But the biggest treat was a hamburger on a bun and a 'long john' sweet roll to follow it down.

Either one would be devoured gladly, but to get *both* was like a round-trip to heaven.

The working men of Sioux Falls were accustomed to taking a coffee break around 10:00 AM, and I knew this. It was, therefore, no accident that I often showed up at my Dad's shop at coffee-break time. As the break time approached, the men of the Sioux Falls Paint and Glass would begin to look at their pocket watches, laying them in the palms of their hands to examine them as if they weren't working quite right. There was almost no project that couldn't be laid aside and attended to later. When the break time came, they would drift to the large doors at the rear of the building that led into the alley behind, and they would start the daily walk to their favorite coffee spot. The Nickel Plate on Phillips Avenue by the E. C. Olson store was closer to the back door, but this was a classier coffee spot than they wanted. The bright chrome stools and tables of the Nickel Plate made them feel less comfortable in their soiled overalls.

The preferred spot was at a well-known established institution in town called the Hamburger Inn. This 12 by 20 bunker-type block building sat next to the alley on Tenth Street. A large window in the front allowed the proprietors, Stan and his partner, to keep tabs on the movements of cars up the highway and to watch for customers. A friendly hand wave was returned by anyone who walked in front of the window. In turn, the cooks could be seen all during the day flipping over the small hamburger patties on the grill by the window. They did a brisk business of selling the best 10-cent burgers in town.

Eating was simple when I was young. Our family had no money to go out to restaurants to dine. Our mother cooked the meals and we ate at home. The first time I was aware of meals being cooked and served by people other than my mother was when our neighbor asked me to wash dishes at his cafe. He was short of help that day, and I helped out. I was paid with a hamburger steak and French fries. What a meal! The second instance of eating out occurred when our 'rich' aunt Geneva took me to Foster's when I was about seven years old and visiting her in Sioux City. Years later my aunt recalled the thrill she had gotten watching me pick out my food. There were so many choices to be made. I heaped with 'one of each'. My eyes were bigger than my stomach, but somehow I managed to put away about two-dollars' worth of food—a considerable sum in those days.

The grocery stores my family mainly patronized were Sunshine and Red Owl mainly. The 'donut maker' machine at the Sunshine at First and Twelfth was the most marvelous invention I had ever seen. A cup of coffee and two donuts for a nickel couldn't be beat. The Red Owl stores had a branch of the Golden Rule Bakery in them, I found out recently. The Golden Rule Bakery at 306 South Phillips was best remembered by me as it had an alley behind it. I would walk down the alley on my way home, hoping someone from the bakery would be loading up pastries and bread into their delivery trucks. Many times I was given a piece of pastry. Heaven! In the 1940s, Dixie Cream Bakery opened on Minnesota Avenue. They had the best glazed donuts in the Midwest. My aunt Hazel worked at the Busy Bee Bakery at 420 Nineteenth Street, and early one morning when I was about seven years old, I visited the bakery. The men had a coffee break and showered me with pastries. Delicious memories! A former neighbor of ours from Seventh Avenue, Mrs. Berg, worked as a clerk at the Patty Ann Bake Shop at 330 South First Avenue (now Sid's Crown Liquor). Sometimes, at the end of the day, she would call our house and inform us that there was day-old pastry and bread that we could have. Usually some of us kids would traipse down and pick up a box of goodies for our family. Mrs. Berg called on one such evening, and my sister, brother, and I went to pick up what she had collected. As we were leaving that night, I informed Mrs. Berg that my mother had died that day. It was a shock to Mrs. Berg, and she was very distressed and apologetic that she had called us that day. Had she known, she would never have had us come down.

Bits and Pieces of life. As I got older, cafes and restaurants began to interest me more. After my mother died, I began working and I 'ate out' more. Many great memories still linger of the considerable variety available at the eating establishments in Sioux Falls. McKennan Cafe, across from Edmund's Grocery, was frequented at lunch time while I was attending Longfellow Grade School my final year. While setting pins at the Sport Bowl, I many times found lunch at the Frisco Lunch (104 North Phillips), Milwaukee Wiener Shop (118 No. Phillips), Cony Island Lunch (128 No. Phillips), and the Nickel Plate (200 North Phillips). Sometimes I would walk down to Sixth Street and get a malt at Bell Creamery (215 W. Sixth) or Dickey's Diner (219 W. Sixth). Dickey's Diner, across from the County Jail, was housed in a unique railroad dining car. If I had more time I went to Kirk's Cafe at Tenth and Main. The S.S. Kresge Company five & dime store at Tenth and Phillips had a long lunch counter and also a hot-dog stand where you could pile on all of the relish on the 'dog' that you wanted, lace it with onions, and tie it all together with ribbons of mustard. Later on when I had more money, the Palace of Sweets at Eleventh and Phillips (later Lemmonds, Minerva's site) was a favorite choice. Their caramel rolls and cherry-cokes were out of this world, a combination that made the waitress shudder when she took the order. While attending Augie, 'Barney' served a fabulous assortment of food at the Augie cafeteria. The 'Huddle' in the basement of the Augie gym was a a hamburger haven, a great place for coffee and conversation. The Barrel drive-in on Minnesota was a frequent destination, as were the many Dairy Queens.

You can have your champagne tastes and caviar dreams, I'll take the savory memories of the Midwest any day.

Beginning in the 1960s, a large number of downtown buildings were torn down and their empty lots used for parking cars. In this 1975 air photo of Sioux Falls, taken by Joel Strasser, the Phillips Avenue that I was familiar with was being razed to clear the way

for a new business district. The Holiday Inn, numerous banks, and other business build-ings were to be constructed in the redevelopment project while Forty-first Street was fast becoming the new shopping area.

MAIN AV S—Contd
208△Frye Maurice J clo clnr
209△Brass Rail liquors
210△Anderson Flower Shop
210½ Maass Ella 1
   △Cogswell Maxine E 2
211△Modern Cleaners & Dyers Inc
212△Shakstad Electric Motor Wks Inc
212½ **Shakstad Block**
Rooms:
   1-2△Negas Harry 2
   3△Eneboe Gusta Mrs 2
   5△Griffith Leon S 1 mus tchr
   7△Harvey Thos 2
Street continued
214△Steele Electric
216△Feay's Friendly Service refrigerators and radios
217*Miller Robt B auto parking
218△Williams Piano Co
   Williams Building
Rooms:
200△S D Education Assn
   S D E A Journal
201△Roessler Christ optometrist
210△Bowring Investment Co
2d fl△Metropolitan Life Ins Co (farm loan dept)
Street continued
219△S F Shopping News
219½ Divney Wm J 2
   △Bogdas Louis G 2
221△Norberg Bros paints
222△Barnett Funeral Chapel
   △Modern Woodmen of America
223△Eat Shoppe
224△RKO Radio Pictures Inc
225½ Dickenson Wm J 1
226△Firestone Stores
   △Nettleton Commercial College
   △Schwietert Chiropractic Clinic
227 Snyder Kenneth A barber
227½△Adamson Yulah Mrs restr
229 Schoneman Hattie restr
231△Eleeson Melvin I fill sta
232△Schletz Paint Supply Co
236△Union Bus Terminal
   △Palace City Bus Lines
   △Overland Greyhound Lines
   △Jack Rabbit Lines (depot)
   Thompson Luella Mrs restr
   W Eleventh intersects
300△United Service Organization
   △Borgen Chevrolet Co
314△Johnson Furn Co
316△American Theatre Supply
318△Paramount Picture Inc
320 Usletten Carl J barber
   Kessler Geo E mus dlr
320½ Kee Jas 2
324-26△OK Tire Shop
324½ O'Hara Frank J 4
330△Electric Motor Repair
334△Sunny Side Dairy
336 Vacant
   W Twelfth intersects

400△Gib & Andy Service fill sta
401△Board of Education (sec ofc)
412△Semm's Magneto Shop
412 **Apartments**
   1 Fortenberry Howard F 2
   2 Nelson Albert G 3
   3 Tine Ralph 2
   4 Tellinghusen Leo 2
   5 Brandt Adolph 2
   6 Sinning Fred 5
   7 Loeffler Lillian Mrs 1
   8 Koval Hilka Mrs 1
Street continued
414△Home Pie Shop
415△Grand Lodge Office and Library (AF&AM)
420△Bale Geo W 13
   W Thirteenth intersects
502△Calvary Cathedral (Episcopal)
507△Miller Funeral Home Inc
509 **Miller Apartments**
Apartments:
   2△Perkins Henry L 4
   3△Lamb Hazel phys
   △Barger Steph F 2
Street continued
511△Sand Simon T 4
512△Stark Leland W F Rev 4
513△VanDeWalle Pharmacy
   △Sercl Wm F phys
   △Reagon Rezin phys
   △Billingsley Paul R phys
515△Policy Holder Natl Life Ins Co
   W Fourteenth intersects
603△Anthony Louise Mrs 8
610△Canaday Edwin A 3 ©
612△Granflaten Adolph F 3
613△Pankow Reynold 2 ©
614△Fellows Ira V 4
615 Koolma Wm 8 ©
616△Renli Merle G 9
617△Knutson Arth 4
618 Nelson Jas P 3
618½△Spencer Albert J 2
619△Miller David W 7 ©
620△Roskeland Magnus 4
621△Lekvold Mabel M 10
623△Spencer Alva M 2
   Duemling Miles H 6
623½△DeLong Edmund C
   Hallquist Einar L 4
630△Freitag Edw 4 ©
632 Hyde Edson H ©
   Bowden Ann Mrs 7
633 Estey Robt F 15
637△Simmons Everett L 2 © dentist
638△Lane Elon W 5 ©
640△Fox Jas W 7 ©
641△Feay Virgil C 2
641½ Fersdahl Jennie Mrs 1
642△LaLonde Norman F 11
643△Wagner Wm G 2 ©
   Egan Frank G 3
643½ Hanneman Russell K 2
   Kelley Leslie J 2
647 Wagner Oscar H 3 © florist

1945

3
The game called football

Football is a game played with eleven players on each team. The seven players positioned on an imaginary line are called linemen and the four players behind them are called backs. Simple thus far, right? The two men on the end of the 'line' are called 'ends' and the appointed general of the team is the 'quarterback', who usually stands behind the center lineman. The center lineman gives the ball to the quarterback so he can direct a 'play', and other men on the line protect and block for the quarterback and backfield players. The three other men in the backfield position themselves in various places so they can make moves to the defenders' area of the field and advance the ball down a field that is fifty yards wide and one hundred yards long, to the 'end zone' where a 'touchdown' is scored, rewarding the team that scores the touchdown with six points. A bonus play is given the scoring team to add one point to the already-earned six points.

Simple, yes? A nice afternoon game to occupy the time of twenty-two boys between lunch and dinner.

Nature being what it is, when the testosterone flows in the male animal and enough adrenaline begins pumping through his body, remarkable achievements could be demonstrated by these athletes during sixty minutes of play.

It became evident before many seasons of football were played that if all the personnel on both teams were pretty much equal in ability, the person coaching the team could, by his personality and expertise, induce his players to play better than the other team. Coaches became all important in the achievement of teams, and many coaches reached God-like status in communities where football became the primary entertainment during the fall season.

However, by the 1950s, the sport of football had advanced way beyond the simple afternoon game and the stage of 'winning' or 'losing' on the field had become a struggle of individuals in quests for more fundamental aspects of life. You could 'find' yourself in these events. These struggles on the fields could open up vistas of educational opportunities for the talented athletic who wanted to obtain a college education, but could not afford to pay his way. I could not afford to go to college. Playing football was the route I took to get my higher education.

Washington High School—1949-50

Washington High School had over two-thousand students in the late 1940s. The school had unique, humongous open halls on the second and third floors of Washington High School that provided a wonderful social

Washington High School offered the key to success in life to me and my classmates in the late 1940s. (photo by Charles Fredricks)

experience for me. Before classes began in the morning and afternoon, almost everybody would congregate in the halls to socialize and get acquainted. At lunch many chose to meet in the school cafeteria, but most brought their lunch and ate in the classrooms that exited into these large halls. In the '50s, due to increased student population, these were converted into classrooms. The students that followed us at Washington High School lost forever a great tradition of community and comradeship that these halls encouraged.

When this people-watching activity in the large hall got boring, a walk throughout the rest of the huge four-story building was undertaken. First one hall was slowly walked, then after a trek up the marble steps to the next floor, that area was explored.

Although it was the biggest high school in the five surrounding states of North and South Dakota, Wyoming, Nebraska, and Minnesota, Washington high school's record in varsity football had been only average in the last few years. The school had more athletes than any other school that they played, but it was evident that something was wrong.

During the summer of 1949, I had had an operation to fix the hernia I had gotten while working at the ice house. Lifting the 300 pound blocks of ice was easy enough, but I slipped while lifting a huge piece of machinery onto the dock outside and that was when I was injured. It wasn't life-threatening and it didn't stop me from weight lifting during my sophomore year. I couldn't participate in football, however. That always struck me as funny: I could repeatedly weight-lift hundreds of pounds of barbells at the YMCA, but I couldn't go out for football.

SIOUX FALLS WARRIORS

Coaches: Bob Burns, Grant Heckenlively

No.	Name	Pos.	Wgt.	No.	Name	Pos.	Wgt.
20	Kolb	Back	136	39	Larson	Back	160
21	Fillmore	Back	150	39	Mortrude	Tackle	155
22	McDowell	Back	149	40	Knudson	Guard	157
23	Artman	Back	135	41	Fliginger	Center	170
24	Carlson	Center	142	42	Friedhoff	End	170
25	Mann	Back	147	43	Enright	Guard	159
26	Bittner	Back	145	44	Darold Erickson	Center	157
27	Kraft	Back	166	45	Enzicker	Guard	168
28	Weiss	Back	157	46	Dick Erickson	End	158
29	Beckman	Back	168	47	Clark	Tackle	170
30	Chuck Erickson	Back	160	48	Brusnighan	Tackle	184
31	Barthalow	Back	140	49	Walton	Guard	164
32	Greenslate	End	150	50	Fredricks	Tackle	179
33	Songstad	Back	151	51	Hutton	Back	161
34	Nelson	Guard	169	52	Donaldson	Guard	205
35	Spear	End	153	53	Smith	Tackle	192
36	Hines	Guard	155	54	Amburn	Tackle	209
37	Elliott	Back	160	55	Peckham	Back	208

Washington High School Football Roster - 1949.

I was ready for my junior year of football, but in 1949, the football coaching situation changed. In 1949 a new football coach from Yankton was hired. His name was Bob Burns and his reputation for toughness and excellent coaching had impressed the school trustees enough that they wanted him to coach the Warriors. Burns had played at South Dakota State on championship teams and, after a stint in the service, he developed an excellent football team at Yankton High School. He came with high recommendations, accomplishments and, most of all, a desire to turn Washington High School football into a winning team. His first appearance was deceptive. He didn't look anything like a championship coach. First of all he was too short, and he looked like a fireplug. He had beady eyes, and he appeared to foam at the mouth slightly when he talked excitedly. Pacing up and down in the field house or the sidelines like a coyote in a cage, he never stopped asking

1949 Varsity Team. A-Squad, L to R. First row: J. Brusnighan, D. Enright, D. Songstad, B. Carlson, J. Artman, P. Kolb, D. Bartholow and E. Fillmore. Second row: G. Heckenlively, line coach, D. Fredricks, J. Nelson, W. Elliott, M. McDowell, W. Morrrude, Dick Erickson, Darold Erickson, B. Kraft, B. Bittner, M. Weiss, C. Erickson and B. Larson, B. Burns, coach. Third row: C. Clark, R. Greenslate, J. Peckham, B. Walton, T. Amburn, B. Friedhoff, D. Smith, J. Fliginger, D. Hutton, B. Donaldson, D. Spear and P. Beckman. 1950 WHS Yearbook

questions of the players. He was never still. It was hard to look him in the eyes, he was so intense. His attitude was so persuasive that you didn't feel you could refuse any command he gave.

"No smoking or drinking. If you are caught doing either, you are off of the team. Period!" His 'no nonsense' attitude made us stand up straighter and think harder. The old coach wasn't this way. This new coach meant business. And business was good. His command of football was extraordinary and his enthusiasm was contagious. We caught the "fever".

The practices were brutal. Calisthenics—over a half-hour of them. Jumping-jacks to warm up, then bend and touch the ground with your fingers, next push-ups, leg-lifts until you felt like dying...but you were too tired to. The two-a-day workouts were nightmares to us. The prevailing attitude at that time was that workouts were meant to be rough and tough and conditioning meant that no water was to be allowed on the field. No water! The sun was boiling us to death and yet no water intake was allowed until the end of the practice. Play after play was run and run again a thousand times. At the end of the practices were a number of 'speed runs' that even though you were exhausted you did not dare 'dog it' or more would be requested by the coaches.

Needless to say, a number of players fell by the wayside and quit after suffering the 'dry heaves'...but not me. I knew I could survive to play. I needed to survive and play football. The demands that football placed on my body and will were exactly what I needed. Here I could demonstrate my athletic skill and, at the same time, release my pent-up frustration and anger at the unfairness of aspects of my life. This socially-accepted outlet for my frustration was exactly what I needed to let off the steam from my boilers. I could hit, punch, and knock over people and obstacles at will, under the rules of course. And they praised me for it. Football... What more could be asked of any sport?

The football season of 1949

The days were mercifully cooler now that school and football season had begun. Practice was after school at Howard Wood Field on East Tenth Street, and it was over two hours long. Most of the players had to walk to the stadium from Washington High School although a few fortunate ones hitched rides with their buddies who had cars. These were mainly seniors. During my junior year I walked to the practice sessions, then I walked home to West Sioux after the practice session. The energy I burned up was enormous. I was always hungry.

The first game of the season began with cross-town rival Cathedral High School. It turned out to be a disaster. The game had all the elements associated with traditional cross-town rivalry. For days all of the conversation in the city focused on this 'big' game. Washington High School could not lose, everyone agreed. All of the players wanted to win in the worst way. When the game was over, WHS had lost... 19 to 7. This was humiliating. I did not play in the contest. I was on the second-string behind Co-captain Tom Amburn.

Coach Burns was very intense during the practices the following week. He continually chewed our butts out trying to find out how to get the best out of us. He had a knack of getting our attention, especially if we missed a block or didn't hustle the way he expected.

The next game was to be played at Brookings. The team had to travel by bus to the stadium. It was a classic fall evening and great for football- cool, but not cold. The game ended with the Burns' men coming out on top with a 13 to 0 win over Brookings. Finally a good win. It was exciting, and exactly what the new coaches, Burns and Heckenlively, had needed. They felt that the team had 'jelled' and that they were now going to be the biggest winners in the Eastern South Dakota Conference. I played in the game for a few short minutes.

And, as a bonus after the game, there was a meal waiting before we returned to Sioux Falls. A meal! A free meal? And in a restaurant. I had never eaten in a restaurant this elegant in my life. I couldn't believe it. And what a meal it was. Salad, with dressing. Bread—rolls. Potatoes, gravy, and a steak. A steak! Man, this was living. A great big steak for myself. During my football career at Washington High School, I looked forward to the games we played *away* from Sioux Falls. Football was not only a rewarding sport...it was nourishing!

Although Brookings fell to WHS by a score of 13 to 0, this was a mighty short winning streak because in the next games against Yankton, East, Central, and Aberdeen, we lost. WHS reverted to its old ways of losing. The school and the town again lost faith in the team.

"You can win, you're better than you've been showing me and the fans." Coach Burns exhorted in his raspy voice that had become even more hoarse by his continual side-line yelling when plays went awry.

Orange Letter Day proved to be the turning point for WHS in 1949. Co-captains Pete Beckman and Tom Amburn rallied the team to new heights. Tailback and quarterback Mick McDowell played over his head behind a line that was finally 'jelling' into a team that would be the hallmark of Coach Burns. Heavily-favored, unbeaten Rapid City came to town, and we defeated them, 6—0, after a hard-fought battle. The team was ecstatic. Burns was pleased. Now things would be different, I thought to myself. Although I had not played in the game, I felt I was part of the victory by just being on the team.

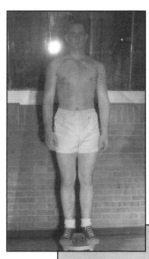

The weightlifting program I undertook at the YMCA in 1948 changed me dramatically by 1950. (left 1949, below 1950)

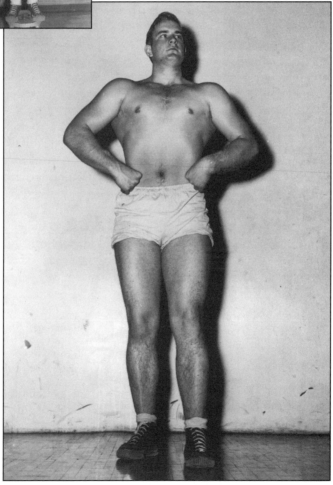

The final two teams we played—Mitchell and Watertown—were defeated. Coach Burns had never lost faith in us or his system. This attitude was the team's salvation. However, the word went out at the end of the season: there would be few monogram letters given out that year. Coach Burns felt that the letters had been given out too freely in the past, and he was determined to make the letter worth something. Letters were to be based on playing time in games. I didn't receive a monogram letter. That hurt. I vowed to myself that I would not go out for football next season.

Washington High School football—1950

I was a senior at WHS in 1950. This was to be my last year of high school. I liked school. I enjoyed the challenge of the books, the teachers, and the opportunity to play football. This was to be it. What life would hold for me after leaving WHS was a complete mystery. This was it, the last year, maybe my final opportunity to stand out from the crowd, to make a name for myself. My buddies had talked my out of quitting football in my senior year. It was a relief to hear that many felt I would make the team and make up for not getting a letter the year before. I had to make as much of my senior year as I could, for I knew this opportunity would never come again.

In the spring, I was offered a job after school at Egger Steel. If I proved out, it could last during the summer. I had been taking drafting classes from Mr. Close for the past three years, and I was very good at drawing buildings, sheds, tools, maps, etc. I loved drawing. The offer to work as a draftsman at Egger Steel came as a surprise. Here was an opportunity to develop my skills at drafting and make some money also. However, it also created a problem for me. If I went to work for Egger Steel, I felt I would not be able to continue football. I didn't feel that I could just start a job and then quit for something like playing football. Decision time was here for me. I wanted to continue football, but the thought of making money was a great incentive to work. But I wanted to play football. By playing football I might get a college scholarship, if I was good enough.

I decided to decline the job. But luck was with me. In the spring I was offered a job working at Wilson Trucking Company on Reid and Eighth Street. I would unload and haul freight from truck to truck on the shipping docks at Wilson's. It was to be hard physical work. Coach Burns was responsible for getting me the offer. He met me in the hall and, after telling me about the job, he said, "It'll get you into shape for football in the fall."

He was right. It was hard, heavy work, and it got me into the best shape I'd ever been in. Every one of my muscles was toned up. It didn't pay very well, however. I worked 60 hours a week and took home less than 50 dollars. Every other week, I had to work on Sunday (70 hours that week), and still I made less than 60 dollars. From this paycheck I had to buy shoes, clothes, food, put gas in my brother's borrowed car that I used to get to work, and when the week was finished, I barely had enough to save for next year's school expenses. If it hadn't been for my sister feeding me at her house, I would have half starved. Vern and Dorothy really kept me going that summer. As the summer progressed, I became convinced that I did not want to do this type of physical labor for a living. I was ready and glad to return to school after this hard summer at Wilson's Trucking Company.

September finally arrived. Everyone was extremely enthusiastic and optimistic when fall practice began. The spirit of the returning team members remained high even after the punishing two-a-day workouts. The winning attitude the team had achieved at the end of the 1949 season appeared to be as strong as the day we turned in our football gear last year. Everyone felt that big things were about to happen. Washington High School was on the edge of greatness.

The many months of body building the previous year at the YMCA had paid off for me. My muscles bulged, and I felt like Hercules. The three hours of workout at the "Y" gym on Mondays, Wednesdays, and Fridays paid off. My large frame had responded favorably to the workout investment. I had taken to lifting weights with the dedication of a divinity student. I had finally found something that I really liked and it satisfied me. As the muscles increasingly responded, the intensity of the workouts increased. I challenged myself to the utmost. Never had I felt so in command of myself and the universe. Weightlifting produced a fabulous feeling of accomplishment and my self-esteem soared. Nothing like this had happened before to me.

I had confidence in myself, but now I had to prove my worth to the coach. I was determined to be on the first-string. In the locker room the first day, however, I found out that the coach had picked Alonzo Smith for the first-string tackle. I was very agitated and upset. 'No way,' I thought. 'What makes the coach think Smith is better? First of all he's a junior. And second of all I'm better. I'll just have to prove it to the coach.'

Our first game with Madison was coming up. I practiced like a man possessed. Coach Heckenlively called Coach Burns over one afternoon to show him how much I had improved from the year before. After the first two or three days of practice, the coach began using both Alonzo and me equally in the practices. Then Alonzo sprained his ankle. I now had the edge. I never looked back. From that time on, my size, strength, and experience made me the number one choice of the coach for the tackle position. That still didn't excuse me from the coach's 'butt chewing' when I didn't perform up to his standards. Being on the first team only intensified them.

When Washington High School took the field at Madison, the team was ready. Sophomore Bob Berguin was the center with Harry Neeley backing

SIOUX FALLS WARRIORS

	NO.	POS.	WT		NO.	POS.	WT
Bartholow	31	G	149	Kraft	30	B	167
Benson	54	T	215	Leach	35	B	147
Berguin	43	C	173	Merrill	32	T	175
Norberg	24	B	141	Neeley	53	T	225
Carlson	23	C	152	Nelsen	34	G	183
Chase	46	G	180	Neuroth	50	B	180
Donaldson	52	C	215	Noel	33	B	155
Dunham	26	G	160	Paulson	48	G	155
Eggiman	37	G	167	Peckham	55	B	209
Erickson, Darold	44	B	168	Pfeifer	21	B	140
Erickson, Dick	41	E	168	Powell	39	E	160
Fredericks	51	T	195	Simpson	29	E	148
Hoover	22	B	133	Skaggs	27	B	136
Hopewell	36	B	152	Smith	25	T	205
Kemmerling	28	E	147	Stockstad	42	B	158
Kirkegaard	47	E	165	Unzicker	45	G	182
Kolb, J	38	E	170	Walton	49	E	169
Kolb, P	20	B	147	Wold	49	E	177

COACHES: Bob Burns and Grant Heckenlively

Washington High School Football Roster - 1950.

him up. Starting ends were Bob Walton and Dick Erickson. Jim Unzicker and I were starting tackles with Francis Chase and George Dunham guards. In the backfield, Paul Kolb, Ken Noel, Darold Erickson, Bill Kraft, and John Peckham carried the load. Our strength lay, however, in the second and third-string players. We were loaded with reserve players like: Sam Pfeifer, Dale Hoover, Jack Nelson, Jim Skaggs, Dwane Leach, Parker Powell, Hal Kirkegaard, 'T.D.' Wold, Bill Simpson, Dick Merrill, Jim Kolb, and Jack Neuroth, to name a few.

The first six games were winners for WHS. Madison was the first win: 20 to 7. After a fabulous night of scoring two touchdowns, our right half-back and potential 'All American' (according to Coach Burns) Paul Kolb dropped the ball on his way to his third touchdown. He also broke his ankle. He was sidelined for the season and became a 'spotter' in the radio booth. This was not, however, a total loss for him as he also was elected marshal for Orange Letter Day, an honor he could not have accepted if he had been playing on the football team.

Next we beat Huron 46 to 0. Peckham, Kraft, Hoover, Wold, Leach, and Skaggs all scored touchdowns. A hard fought game gave us the edge over Brookings—20 to 12. Coach Burns needed to beat Yankton. We blanked them 46 to 0 with Noel and Kirkegaard scoring twice. Sioux City East gave the Orange and Black a scare by scoring first, but WHS got rolling and beat them, 26 to 7. The Sioux City Central score ended up 20 to 12 in favor of WHS.

Five thousand fans packed the stadium on the East Side for the Homecoming game with Aberdeen. Ron Greenslate acted as OLD Master of Ceremonies. Paul Kolb was the OLD Marshal, with Jim Wylie, Courtney Anderson, Jack Hoffmann, and Kenny Anderson as Royalty. Patty Masters was his queen, with Mary Ann Davis, Bonnie Beck, Pat Rustad and Veloy Hawkey as Royalty. John Peckham electrified the fans with a 64-yard scoring run. Aberdeen lost by 27 to 6. Despite our lop-sided victories, the fans continued to pack the stadium just to see Coach Burns' exciting team.

Washington High School now had ten wins in a row since the previous year when we had upset Rapid City six to zero in Sioux Falls. Now we were to meet them again, but this time on their turf in Rapid City. The game was being touted as the game of the unbeaten titans. It was to be their homecoming and, on top of that, Dad's Day. Although there was no official state championship, everyone knew this was it. Rapid City was unbeaten this year, and they were out to avenge their loss of last year. They weren't going to let any advantage pass in order to defeat the highly ranked Washington High School. The pride of both teams was on the line.

After an all-school rally in the auditorium, our team of thirty players left on Thursday morning. It was a rousing send-off, and we boarded the bus confident we would beat the Cobblers. In Pierre we held a workout at the local school, and then the team spent the night at a hotel. Many of the players complained to the coach that they were tired. "Must be the elevation," the coach confided to his assistant. "Maybe we should have brought some oxygen with us."

WHS meets Rapid City for the 'State Championship'

When the Warrior team entered the School of Mines stadium on Friday night, they were met with a horrendous sound of car horns. The Rapid City supporters kept blinking the lights of their cars on and off.

"They're pulling out all of the stops tonight," Coach Burns told us. "The stadium is packed with eight-thousand parents, and it's surrounded on three sides with autos. Rapid City is out to beat us tonight. They're looking for blood. We'll just have to prove them wrong."

During warm-ups, I felt almost sick, as did many of the other players.

"Has to be the altitude," Coach Burns again confided to his coaches. "We'll have to substitute players early and often," he said. "This may be a

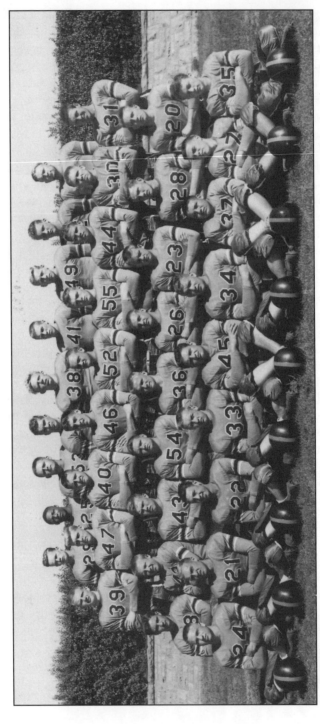

1950 Varsity Football Team. A-Squad, L to R. Front Row: D. Bowen, S. Pfeifer, D. Hoover, K. Noel, J. Unzicker, J. Nelson, R. Eggiman, J. Skaggs and D. Leach. Second row: D. Paulson, B. Stockstad, B. Berguin, D. Benson, D. Hopewell, G. Dunham, B. Carlson, C. Kemerling and P. Kolb. Third row: P. Powell, H. Kirkegaard, D. Wold, F. Chase, B. Donaldson, J. Peckham, D. Erickson, B. Kraft and D. Bartholow. Fourth row: B. Simpson, A. Smith, H. Neeley, J. Neuroth, J. Kolb, Dick Erickson, B. Walton, D. Merrill and D. Fredricks. 1951 WHS yearbook

long night. I should have brought them here a few days before to get them acclimatized. Too late now though."

Bob Berguin started at center. As a sophomore he had more than proved that he was an excellent player, and he helped WHS into the winning column each year he was there. The rest of the line—Bob Walton, Francis Chase, George Dunham, Jim Unzicker, and Dick Erickson and I were experienced and confident. Darrell Erickson was the quarterback, backed up by John Peckham, Dwight Hoover, and Kenny Noel.

Game time!

The kickoff went to WHS, but we couldn't get going and we had to give the ball up to Rapid City. Rapid City scored on the first play they tried. We were already behind by a score of 7 to 0. My legs failed to obey a direct order from my brain. They felt like lead, and I could hardly run. Our team was out of it, but somehow we had to hype ourselves up and play. It was going to be a real struggle to keep up with the Rapid City players. After a fumble by Rapid City, Hoover passed to Erickson to score. The after-point was missed. Score 7 to 6. In the second quarter, 'Crazy Legs' Thayer of Rapid City led a march to score and after, missing the extra point, Rapid City led 13 to 6. Washington High immediately retaliated on the kickoff by scoring on a 65-yard pass from Hoover to Noel. Again the after-point was missed and WHS trailed by 13 to 12. After an exchange of ball possession, the ball was fumbled and Rapid City recovered. They scored and led 20 to 12 at the half-time. We were still in the game but barely, when the half-time show began.

The third quarter resulted in a stalemate. Dick Thayer scored in the final quarter and Rapid City led by 27 to 12. After a score by John Peckham, Hoover scored the extra point and WHS trailed by 27 to 19. A slight glimmer of hope. WHS was on Rapid City's 25-yard line and driving for a touchdown when the final gun sounded.

We sustained a 27 to 19 loss to a very strong Rapid City team, a team that obviously could play better in mountain air than the WHS fellows from the flatlands. Afterwards we all jumped into the Rapid City swimming pool to cool off. It had been a tough season up to this point. The season ended with eight wins, one loss, and one 13 to 13 tie with Watertown at a bone-chilling 13-degree-temperature contest.

The start of a football dynasty at WHS

In 1950 Washington High School had won the Eastern South Dakota championship for he first time since the great Dan Dworsky played in 1944.

This season was to be the start of a 37-game winning streak by the Orange and Black. In 1951, WHS won every game. John Peckham, Ike Hoover, Don Renner, Jack Neuroth, Dick Wold, Jim Kolb, and the other members of the team were unstoppable. The undefeated year was repeated again in 1952. WHS had begun a victory march that would just keep going and going.

This year of athletic success was the best medicine I could ever have hoped for. All of my pain and effort had paid off. Hard work, self-sacrifice, and faith were ideals to live by. The world was my oyster now. I walked taller than I ever thought was possible.

....

Still, I was not totally satisfied with my accomplishments.

*"If you want to **make** something of yourself, you have to **do** something", I said to myself. "There are no free rides."*

Self-motivation, I heard somewhere, is the key to success, plus some common sense and a little intelligence. I think my father told me that once. He never gave me much advice except maybe this bit of wisdom. At the time it seemed profound, and I remembered it. I wonder if he even knew what he had said. He never succeeded in the way I wanted to succeed. He was always working to feed the family. Too damn many kids to feed. All of the time he worked, nights, weekends, all of the time. Never home enough to spend time with us kids. A few times we would go rabbit hunting or pheasant hunting along the road, but that was to get food to feed the family. He was always working. He never had time to enjoy himself. Just worked.

I didn't want to end up like that. But what can I do here? There's nothing for me here. God forbid, maybe there's nothing for me anywhere.

Man, I need to succeed, but how? I have potential. I am smart, a go-getter, and a hard-worker. Those are my abilities. Maybe I should be happy with just that, but I keep feeling the need to do something more. But what? What can I do to fulfill my inner needs and also make some money? Without money I know I won't be able to make it. Not a whole lot of money but enough to buy a car and a house maybe. I don't want to go through life just eating and breathing and paying the bills. Something is driving me and I know I will need more than material goods to get to my destination. I'll need a map, a life-plan, for the road ahead.

4
A reunion – old buddies and friends

I pulled up to the curb and stopped my car. I sat inside, not moving, just looking around. It seemed unreal to me. Here I was, back where I was born, but I felt like a stranger. Did I belong here anymore?

I was parked on a slight hill. Below me, close to the corner of Forty-first and Lake, was a small one-story bunker-like building. Must be the locker-room for the football players, I thought. Cars were parked on the street around it, and, as I sat there, another car drove up. Two husky fellows got out, slammed the car doors and jogged toward the building.

To my right was a practice field with a running-track surrounding it. A few runners were jogging on it in groups of two. In the center of the field there were men in football uniforms doing push-ups, stretching their legs, throwing footballs back and forth, with a few standing around watching the others.

I had just arrived from California the day before, and, after finding out that football practice was scheduled for this afternoon, I decided to see what was going on. Off to my right was a newer two-story building that people had told me about. It must be the new Elmen Athletic Building, I thought to myself. Nice building. Must have cost a fortune. I went to high-school with the Elmen boys, Jim and Bob, although I didn't know Bob as well as I did Jim. Jim had been in some of my classes at Washington High School and at Augie when I began there in the early 1950s. Those boys must have done pretty well to have a building named after them.

The sun was shining and the car was getting warm. I had procrastinated long enough. It had been a long time since I had left Augie, so I didn't expect to know anyone around here. Still, I felt compelled to see what was going on. Maybe reliving some of my old football experiences while watching practice would satisfy me and help lighten this heavy nostalgic feeling.

....

"Burns is the only reason I am back this year. I planned on going to Kansas University or Colorado U to finish, but I figured this could be the best year yet for me in college. About time we had a good coach at Augie. It's been hard as hell being on a team that you knew was going to lose almost every game. Losing is bad, but it's really humiliating being on a losing team that you know has good talent, especially when you know that you can do better if things were a little different. That coach we had last year was as bad as my Army coach. Bullheaded, inept, slow to react, and with very little imagination. We'd better do something this year.

45

I need to go out a winner. With you back, and some of the junior transfers that I hear are coming, we could have a hell-of-a-team, if the coach lets us play."

"Burns will let us play. I talked to him last week, and he is really hot to get going, and he's let everybody know that he not only wants to win, but win big. And he will... Everybody in town that I've talked to is really excited about his coming to Augie to coach. Nobody ever expected him to make the move to Augie. Maybe State or the University, but not Augie, especially with the reputation it's had for the past ten years. Augie's been the doormat for too many years, and it'll be an uphill battle all of the way. From last place to first place, that's what I want. Man, we've got the material to really go all out. All we need are a few breaks and some luck. We also need a little more depth. Everybody will have to play a lot, but we can do it. What do you think, Fred?" I had been staring out of the window into the dim darkness as Walton was speaking.*

I played my last football game for this college in 1956, under Coaches Burns and Rist. Since then, thousands of students and players had passed through Augie's doors and made their way out into the world. Me included. Now I was retired after teaching science in California for almost 35 years...but something was pulling me back to this place, my roots in life. Would anything be familiar to me, or would everything be totally different? I walked past the locker-room building and across the grass toward the goal posts at the end of the practice field.

I felt alone and kind of sheepish. Why was I here? Just to look, I told myself...but I knew there was more to it than that simple answer.

I stood for a while looking over the field and observing some of the moves being made by the players on the field.

Someone walked up behind me and stopped.

"Fredricks? Aren't you Dick Fredricks?" I heard a voice half questioning and half-answering.

I turned around and looked at the speaker. The sun was at my back and I had trouble getting a good fix on him, but there was something about the person that I recognized. "Yes, I'm Fredricks. Do I know you?" I asked.

"Bob. Bob Kirshman. We worked at Woolworth's one summer. I rode on your motorbike with you up by the Cathedral. Remember that summer? 1948 or 1949?"

Remember it? I sure did. I bought a motorbike after the Second World War, while I was a freshman at Washington High School and working at the Sport Bowl. One day Bob and I took a ride on it, Bob behind me on the bike. Somehow he got his shoe caught in the spokes of the rear wheel. His foot was O.K. but some of the spokes got twisted a little. Could still ride the bike, but I never let anybody ride on the bike with me again.

"Yeah. I do remember. That was a long time ago. How are you doing?"

The conversation had continued for only a few minutes when another man with some equipment for the players came up to us.

"Fredricks?" he burst out. "Well, I'll be darned. What are you doing here in Sioux Falls?"

....

And so began my re-introduction to Sioux Falls. Bob and an almost-forgotten-boyhood friend, Hildar 'Hill' Monger, were now retired from the post office and working at Augie as equipment managers for the football team. "Fourteenth Street, remember where Beadle School was?, I lived a half-block away from it," Hill was saying. "I was part of the 'Sixth Avenue Gang,'" he laughed.

"Yeah. You guys used to scare the hell out of me when I walked by your neighborhood. I was born to the south of you. On Seventeenth Street and Eighth Avenue. Remember?"

In the 1930s, the neighborhood around Seventeenth Street and Eighth Avenue was a kid's paradise to play in. There were great open spaces everywhere. To the east lived the Gartner family in their white, two-story house. This was the biggest, neatest house around. To the east of their house was the biggest temptation that could be offered to any boy—the Great Northern Railroad tracks. These tracks had been built for the north-south main line of the Great Northern. In addition to these tracks there were a number of siding tracks. These were used for the switching of boxcars and temporary storage while they were being formed into larger trains for distant destinations. All this activity along the tracks fascinated me. The steam trains were most impressive and mysterious. Where did they came from and where were they were going? The steam that occasionally sprayed out of the engine was awesome. You kept your distance. The engineer always seemed to know our whereabouts and if we ventured too close, a flume of steam would come hissing out at us. We could see the engineer roar with laughter. He knew he had scared the hell out of us.

"Yeah, I remember. You and your family went to Beadle School for a while. I remember your brother Chuck the best. You moved up to Third Avenue in the '40s, didn't you?"

I tried to remember where Fourteenth and Seventh Avenue was—Beadle School I began counting streets from the Post Office on Twelfth Street and Phillips where I had worked after college graduation in 1957 meanwhile Hill had moved on in his conversation.

"Your old neighborhood by Seventeenth Street is gone now. Egger Steel is using most of it for a parking lot, and McKennan Hospital owns the rest. Your house has been torn down and there's a park-like lawn area there now. The house you lived in on Third Avenue is still there, but it's been remod-

THIRD W—Contd
305 Mofle Raymond 4
909△Marion Clarence G 5 ⓪
924△Oswald Anthony C 6 ⓪
　　　N Menlo av intersects
1000 Dittman Walter C 3 ⓪ pntr
　　　Terrace pl begins
1006△Allen Donald S 4 ⓪
1008△Tennyson Wilfred A 4 ⓪
1010△Lange Cath Mrs 3 ⓪
　　　N Grange av intersects

THIRD AV N—From 500 E Sixth av
　　north to beyond E Fifth
433△Bingham John 6
430 Strickland John W 2
431 Old Style Lager Co
　　　E Fifth begins
528 Nelson Andrew C 1 ⓪
530 Light Bros Co (junk yds)
531 Skelly Oil Co bulk plant
625 Grotjohn Claus F 1 ⓪
626 Digre Carl A 1
627 Bye Harriette M 1 ⓪
629 Anderson John 2

THIRD AV S—From ½ block north of
　　400 E Twelfth south to city limits
　　(not open between 1400 and E
　　Thirty-first)
321△Dresser Lee E 5
324△Adams Jas E 7 trucking
328 Wenham Chas 2
　　　E Twelfth intersects
400 Collins Apts
Apartments:
　　1△Harris Verne M 4
　　2△Smook Harm J 4
　　3 Larsen Jens 2
　　4△Cornish Wendell E 3
Street continued
405△Houk Neil D 9 ⓪
406△White Ralph A 3
407 Aldrich John M 4
408△Schultz Elmer 2
409△DeBelts Albert 4
410△Collins Louise H Mrs 3 ⓪
412△Thickett Harold L 3 ⓪
　　Thickett Jos shoe repr
412½ Pettijean Harold 2
414 Runyan Maude Mrs
417△Kohler Roseanna Mrs 1 ⓪
419△Mitchell Rolette Mrs 4 ⓪
420 Tracy Grace Mrs 1 ⓪
421△Johnson Alex 6 ⓪
422△Fallon Wm J 3
　　　E Thirteenth intersects
501 Sunwall Kaleb 3
503△Krueger Zelda R Mrs 4
503½△Kohnen Wm 4
508△Savage John H 2 ⓪
510△Frost Laura Mrs 4
512△Weidenbach Eug A 2 ⓪
516△Turner Russell S 3
517△Jacobson Roy F 7 ⓪
518△Moss Albert 5
522△Rooks John 2 ⓪

523 Vacant
　　　E Fourteenth intersects
605 Rogness Henry A 2 ⓪
608△McDowell Louis A 3
610 Saunders Dallas A 8
611△O'Rourke Idelle M 5 ⓪
611½ Vacant
612△Christopherson Cora Mrs 3 ⓪
613 Rea Earl M
616 Dahl Martha O Mrs 1
　　△Calvert Tom M 2 pntr
618△Crammond Jas L 2 ⓪
618¾△Kolaas Clifford B 2
620△Thoms Walter G 7 ⓪ auto
　　repr
630△Bale Okie D Mrs 3 ⓪
632△Bale Robt H 6 ⓪
636△Welliever Opal Mrs 3
　　　E Fifteenth intersects
703△Brown W Lester 7 ⓪
703½△Welby Jeniece 1
707△Peck Miles E 3 ⓪
719△Young Horace G 5
720△Buesen Tillie Mrs 3 ⓪
721△Gerry John T 3 ⓪
721½△Wells Ella L Mrs 1 ⓪
　　　CStPM&ORy crosses
722△Doughty Chas T 3 ⓪
726 Anderson Chris 4
728△Monson Josephine H Mrs 1 ⓪
733△Hanger Iver B 5 ⓪
735△Thompson Floyd S 7
738△Fauske Constance Mrs 2 ⓪
739△Thomson Ralph K 2 ⓪
　　△Hunt Dora Mrs 2
　　△Spars Lorraine 2
　　△Pitkanen Geo 3
　　△Thomson Broom Factory
rear Royce Muriel Mrs 3
740△Johnson Emma Mrs 5 ⓪
741△Fredericks Ada M 2
742△Myhra Harry B 4
743△Timmerman Linda C 2 ⓪
744△Famestad Michl A 4 ⓪
745△Mulvey Marie W Mrs 2 ⓪
746△Carnahan Wilbur F 3
750△Heinson Carl W 5 ⓪
756 Haugland Stanley O 4
757△Schumacher Hans J 3 ⓪
758△Tunge Paul H 7 ⓪
760 Stephens Jennie Mrs 1
761△Houg Laurits I 3 ⓪
　　Bratberg Sanford O 3
762△Goldie Chas M Rev 4 ⓪
762½ Rathman Cora Mrs 1
763△Fredricks Elmer H 10 ⓪
765△Bennett Myron J 2
901△Weide Elvin A 3 ⓪
902 Vacant
906△Fjellin Ralph 2 ⓪
907△Shoop Loren I 4 ⓪
910△Hastings Thos J 2 ⓪
911△Lacome Ernest L 3 ⓪
914△Voss Alf D 5 ⓪
915△Erdman Adolph W 4 ⓪
918△Burns John M 4 ⓪

48

eled. You'd never recognize it. I used to live across the street from it when I first got married. "

"Boy, you have a good memory. It's been so long since I lived in those two houses. Yeah, I left Third Avenue in 1947, after my mother died. That place was in the heart of the Galesburg Addition."

From the front porch I could see a poster hanging from the tree in front of Mrs. Goldie's house. She's at it again, I thought. The pioneer West produced many hard-drinkers and alcoholics. Conditions were far from comfortable and the country did not have a lot of cash money floating around. Wages were low and the lack of cash put a great strain on the man of the house to adequately feed and clothe a large family. Many could not even afford what we now call the basic necessities. Every town in the West abounded in businesses that offered some relief from this stressful situation, if only for a few hours. Liquor stores and bars many times outnumbered other businesses in the young western towns. It was inevitable that the philosophy of the churches would clash with the drinking of alcohol. Drinking was looked upon as a grave weakness and a sin put on earth by the Devil. It was wrong to drink and it was condemned by church-going members. It had to be eliminated. The Women's Christian Temperance Union and other organizations sprang up to confront and correct this problem. Well-meaning women and men held meetings in their homes to warn of the evils of drinking alcohol. Any and all forms of drinking were wrong. Even advertisements in magazines were to be cut out and destroyed whenever you had the opportunity. You were never, never to drink alcohol or you would become an alcoholic and ruin your life and bring shame to your family. 'Lips that touch liquor will never touch mine'. When the meetings for the kids were finished at Mrs. Goldie's house, cookies were served with milk to drink. Thousands of such meetings were held throughout the United States by the W.C.T.U. members.

I never drank a beer until I was in the Army. Mrs. Goldie had gotten to me early enough in life.

"Downtown Sioux Falls" Hill continued, "has changed quite a bit since you were here. Nothing's left that we knew. Everything's moved out to Forty-first Street: the Empire Mall, Western Mall, Sam's, hotels, motels, restaurants, they're all there. Remember when this area was the end of town? Used to be a grocery store at the corner of Thirty-third and Grange where the bus stopped. This was pasture then. Augie had only about five-hundred students when you were here. You lived in West Sioux when you went to Augie after high school, didn't you?"

"Lived there the last three years of high school and the first year and a half while at Augie," I replied.

When I was 15 years old, a move to 1720 West Madison Avenue was necessary. My sister, Dorothy and her husband Vern had been taking care of the fam-

ily. My bother-in-law had taken a job in western South Dakota on a road-con-struction crew so my dad bought a house in West Sioux for those who were still at home. The years at Fifteenth and Elmwood had been too short a time to develop relationships as strong as Third Avenue had, so this move was easier. And the ties with friends at Washington High School remained a strong bond in my life.

So many outside activities were keeping me busy. Work at the Sport Bowl and studies in High School had widened my world. I had acquired many more bud-dies and acquaintances beyond my immediate family and they were part of my life now. The move to West Sioux was added another dimension to my life. The small one-story, two-bedroom, brown-shingled house at 1720 Madison Street was well isolated from the rest of the community. Down the dirt road to the west about five blocks was Brockhouse's Grocery Store and a number of small businesses that comprised the center of West Sioux. One block to the east stood the abandoned hospital barracks of the Army Radio Training Base, remnants of the just-com-pleted war. They would be pressed into use as an elementary school in a couple of years as West Sioux was increasing its population rapidly. The fence to the base had been knocked down, and part of the black-topped army road was being used as a short cut to Burnside. This shortcut to downtown saved a longer route around Elmwood and then east on Burnside.

My sister and her husband along with their two children, David and Ruby, moved back to Sioux Falls in 1949. I was now living alone in the house while finishing school at WHS. They parked their trailer house on the adjacent vacant lot until they could buy a house in West Sioux at 1120 North Elmwood. Without the generosity of Vern and Dorothy I would have starved to death. The times were lean and there was little food in my house. I always managed to be around their place at meal time.

Later North Western Avenue would be built here, the barracks removed and business encouraged to use the area as a business park. The area surrounding my home would be designated for use as a recreation complex in the late 1950s and its isolation altered. McCart Fields were developed to the south and, after razing the house I lived in, the Sioux Falls Public School Central Service complex was built on the site.

Augustana football of the 1950s

What a stroke of luck. I had returned to Augie and right off I ran into two of my childhood buddies. You can't get any luckier than that. As soon as we started talking on the practice field, a whole rush of memories began to fill my brain. The old Augie football 'Viking' stadium I had played in is torn down now; graduation from Washington High School in January 1951; Longfellow Grade School; working at Weatherwax Clothing Store on Phillips Avenue in 1951; leaving Sioux Falls the day after marriage in 1958. Everything was coming back to me at once. A few minutes before, I had felt

KSOO SIOUX FALLS NBC KELO

MADISON W—Contd
2042 Mackey Dora Mrs 2 ◎
    N Holly av begins
    N Elmwood av intersects
    N Lincoln av intersects
    Northwest ends
2210△Thomas Food Market
    Post Office (sub sta)
2304△West Sioux Falls Grocery
    Wade Elmer J meats
    △West Soo Lockers
2304½ Wade Elmer J 2
2306 Masur Jerome E barber
2308△Walker & Daggett restr and
    beverages
2315△Loucks Elmer R 6 ◎
    N Garfield av intersects
2400△Elmwood Service Station
    Walheim Andrew A 1
2404 Arvidson Carl H 4
2406△Schryver Roy 2 ◎
2413 Baker Wm B 3 ◎
2417△Witt Arth W 2
2419 Brech Elmer 3
2421△Feay Alex N 4 ◎
    N Kiwanis av intersects
2501△Feay's Garage
2512△Isakson Loraine R 2 ◎
    Baron Lyle W 5 ◎
    Harlem av intersects
2811△Srong's Inc Florists greenhse
    △Hartsook Willis E 4
2812△Axsell Fred H 4 ◎
    Haley av intersects
    Helen av intersects
    City limits
2914 Big Sioux Tourist Camp
    △Borneman Mary A Mrs 1 ◎
    Sioux River
2921△Miller Elmer L 3
3016 Wendt Henry 2 fill sta
3300△West Sioux Lbr Co
end△Concrete Materials Co plant and
    quarry
    Minnehaha County Fairgrounds

MAIN AV N—From 200 W Ninth north
    beyond W Walnut
101△Lunchette System The restr
    △Sioux Falls Production Credit
    Assn
    △Natl Farm Loan Assn
    △Federal Land Bank
103 Wide Awake Shoe Shop
104△Lincoln Hotel
105△Eagle Bar The
106△Kreiscr Surgical Supply Co
107 Bozarth Casper M typewriters
    △Smith Clifford F plmbr
    △Argus Barber Shop
107½△A Y P Hotel
109△Argus-Leader The (daily)
    △Argus-Leader Co Inc The
    △Associated Press The
110△Ritz Cafe

113△Brown's Permanent Wave Shop
    Bailey-Glidden Building
Rooms:
    1△Kutil Marie Mrs 2
    2△Kundert Everett W 2
2d fl△Bailey Voorhees Woods & Fuller
    lawyers
    △Bailey C O Estate
    3 Harris Iola Mrs 2
    4 Flanders John 1
    5 Strange Jas W 1
    6 Berven Tillman C 2
Street continued
114△Day & Nite Garage
115△Builders Supply Co
115a△Pixley Appliance Co
116 Humm Joe lndry
116½ Humm Joe 1
117△Victory Service Center
    Mulder Rudolph 2
118△Bell Clifford L 2d hd furn
120△Hinterlong Furn Co
120½△Mandskor Hall
    Minnehaha Mandskor Singing
    Society
121△Costello Co farm loans
123△Boston Lunch
124 Mickey's Bar Colonial
125△State Liquor Store
126△Soo Lunch
127△Bruner Ernest W billiards and
    beer
    Bruner Orlo E barber
128△Ace Furn Co
130△Chord's Cafe
    Chord Robt 3
131△Western Surety Co ins
132△Brink Hardware
135 **Western Surety Building**
Rooms:
201△Brown Ferdinand V dentist
203 Parliman & Parliman lawyers
204△Hanson Hans lawyer
205△Lacey W Gregg ofc
    △Lacey Chas lawyer
    △Lacey Eileen lawyer
207 Darst Luther E ins
208△Frank Eug B real est
209△Brewster Chas E lawyer
210△Nilsson Mercantile Co
212△Kean Lawrence J lawyer
    Kean Adjustment Co
216 Vacant
218 Vacant
219△Berry Chas R real est
301 Vacant
302 Hills of Rest Memorial Park
    (sls ofc)
303△Mundt John C lawyer
305△Smith Louis H lawyer
306-08△Feyder Theo N lawyer
    △Peck Miles E lawyer
309 Vacant
312△Delbridge Carelton J lawyer
    △Maher Jerry E lawyer
    △Johnson Theo R lawyer

totally dumb for thinking that anybody would ever remember me back here in the Heartland. All that had dramatically changed and my head was now swimming as I tried to remember the times and events that Bob and Hill were both throwing out for conversation.

I've got to see all of this change, I told myself. Got to find my 'old' home-town. "Maybe you can show me the town when and if I get time, Hill," I said. "I won't be here very many days but I'll try to get away. If you have the time."

"Right, O.K. Have you been to the quarterback club meeting on Mondays? Out at the American Legion on Burnside—not too far from West Sioux. You've got to go next time. Hey, follow me and I'll show you the place here." Bob said as he beckoned to the building behind us.

Stepping inside revealed the dressing rooms that smelled of sweat. It was a smell you get used of when you go out for any sport. "The facilities here are relatively new," Hill was saying.

"When I was at Augie we had our dressing room in the Old Brick Gymnasium that had the boiler rooms of the heating plant in the basement," I replied. "Winter or summer, it was always warm, and most times too hot. Never enough room for the team, but it served the purpose."

"Bet you never had it this good when you were playing." Hill said.

"Hell," I burst out, "When I started playing in 1947, over at Howard Field on the East Side, we still had leather helmets. The next year we got plastic helmets. Get hit square on the head and the helmet would break. No padding inside either."

"This building has a lot of room. In here is the equipment cage," and he pointed as we walked. "Over here is the room where the equipment is washed. I do that. This part of the building probably has two or three times as much room as you had in the old Gymnasium."

"Let's look at the weight room." and Bob beckoned me toward the door.

As we walked into the weight room, Bob introduced me to a couple of the coaches. They were friendly and well groomed men.

I stood and watched the men going through different stages of exercise with the weight.

"In the early 50s weight programs were non-existent." I said matter-of-factly. "There wasn't a bar-bell on the Augie campus or at Washington High School. Coach Burns, the football coach at Washington High School, stopped me one day in the hall and inquired about my health. I was going out for football in the fall and he was new at the school - his first year. 'Better stop that weight lifting over at the 'Y', Fredricks' he said. 'It'll just slow you down and make you muscle-bound.' I listened attentively but I knew I wasn't going to quit. I now weighed one hundred eighty pounds and had too much energy. The YMCA had acquired a bar-bell set that year and had set aside a room to work out in. Dale Fellows and a number of others became interested in gymnastics and weight lifting and had started a sort of club three nights a week. I started lifting weights in the evenings and acquired a great deal of strength rapidly. I loved it. It was a self-competitive sport and I liked the challenge even though the benefits of weightlifting had not become accepted in the schools. "Against Burn's advice I kept lifting, and the following year I made first-string on the football team. Although Burn's was a good coach, I proved him wrong on this point." Now it's interesting to see this weight room when in the early 50s there was not even a barbell on Augie's campus.

....

"Hey, Fred, I've got something that you might like to read. It's in my desk in the next room. You've got to take a look at this 1956 newspaper article I brought out to show the coach. I was looking through a bunch of papers the other day that I had put in a box at home and saved. It's from the 1950s. You were on the 1956 Augie football team, right?" Hill said as he led me out of the weight room.

"Yes. That was Bob Burn's first year at Augie. Let me look at it." I replied.

ABOUT-FACE MADE IN AUGIE FOOTBALL
by Dee Chambers Associated Press Sports Writer

LOOP DOORMAT BECOMES POWER

The Augustana College football team has had newspaper readers wondering if sports writers weren't getting team names confused.

It seemed impossible that a team which had apparently become addicted to losing should loom as a potential champion of the North Central Conference.

How could a school that has lost 50 games and won only 9 in the conference in the last 10 years suddenly blossom as a title contender?

More broadly, does this herald a new look for Augustana College, a staid church school long known for its accent on academic pursuits and its small-college intimacy?

Both questions are warranted.

Since the war, the school has been outscored 1,702 points to 451 in the conference. It had failed four out of the last ten years to win even a single conference victory. It had finished last or deep in the standings every year since 1942, when it tied for the conference title.

Yet this year, it is running second behind undefeated but once-tied Morningside, which Augie plays Saturday. And it has knocked off two teams it had never in history defeated before: Iowa Teachers and South Dakota State.

WHAT HAS HAPPENED?

Since the team that is winning this year is essentially the same as the one that didn't last year, there's argument as to what has happened. Most agree that it is some combination of the following factors:

New Head Coach Bob Burns, who brought a 55-8 record with him from Washington High School here ... the intricate, multiple offense that Burns devised and installed ... new Line Coach Marv Rist, a mathematician turned coach whose facility for analysis is said to be the key to the line's habit of making the same mistake only once ...

Quarterback Phil Nelson of Minneapolis, a virtual nobody last year but termed "the best back of the conference" by an opposition coach recently ... the psychology of being the underdog ... an amazing spirit on the part of team members ... and luck.

The new offense probably stimulated spirit as well as give the team a deadly weapon this fall. It uses a spread unbalanced line, a flanker (alternating weak and strong ends), and the other backs in a loose split T line up. From it, the team can shift to get the power of a single wing, the passing potential of a spread and the deception of a split T. It employs a potential of 200 plays. The team sometimes will shift as many as four times on a single play.

Nelson's emergence has been vital, Burns says. The 195-pound back has won two games with his conversion toe, is a steady and accurate punter, can pass long and short and is fast and powerful afoot. He also has a knack for analyzing the opposition, both defensively and offensively.

TELLS A STORY

Being underdogs is a boost, Burns asserts, and tells a story to illustrate. He said he heard players of South Dakota University arguing about which of them would score the most touchdowns against Augie.

"So we opened the door a little so the kids (Augie) could hear it," Burns tells.

"The louder it got, the quieter our kids got until you could hear a pin drop. When we told the kids to get out on the field, they almost tore the door off."

They won 14-13.

Burns agrees that luck is important, especially since injuries could ruin him. He says that despite being outweighed 20 to 25 pounds in each game, his starting eleven—except for the ends—usually plays all 60 minutes.

As to whether the Vikings can keep on winning this year, no one will say. There's tough Morningside, then one more conference opponent: last-place

North Dakota University. It's a tougher team than its ranking indicates, and Burns isn't promising a thing.

Next year, the Vikings will have lost most of this year's starters and Burns says he hasn't found another Nelson among the juniors and sophomores. Hard recruiting has given the school what Burns calls the best frosh team it has ever had, and they'll be ripening next year. But you can't win with sophomores, Burns says.

Later though, Burns and Rist figure they will have a real crackerjack outfit, and they intend to be a permanent force to be reckoned with once their rebuilding program shows up on the field.

Sioux Falls Argus-Leader Thursday Oct. 25, 1956

....

"Hill," I cried out loud, "this is incredible. You may not believe this but I just put together a little story about the 1956 Augie football team. A full-sized book. Pictures and everything. Here take a look at these statistics I put together.

Augustana Football Records to 1956

	SDState vs. Augie	SDU vs. Augie	IowaST vs. Augie
1947	33-12	--	39-0
1948	20-6	39-13	34-0
1949	28-0	47-13	49-0
1950	20-12	33-14	24-13
1951	58-7	54-7	67-7
1952	47-6	62-18	47-0
1953	55-0	33-0	39-13
1954	68-0	33-6	50-0
1955	28-0	35-18	28-7
1956	20-21	12-14	6-13
	NDU vs. Augie	**Morningside vs. Augie**	**No.Dak.State vs. Augie**
1947	13-7	7-14	7-13
1948	13 13	14-21	14-6
1949	21-0	26-7	13-7
1950	27-7	60-6	6-0
1951	Canceled	25-0	0-12
1952	33-21	33-0	13-24
1953	35-0	19-0	34-18
1954	39-0	26-0	6-6
1955	32-19	40-7	0-13
1956	14-26	21-13	42-7

....

"I started writing about history in California a few years ago, and I put together a little story about Bob Burn's and the first year he was at Augie. He was my high school football coach at Washington High School so I knew him when he came to Augie in my senior year. He really stirred up Augie and the Heartland in 1956 when he pulled off one of the best winning years that Augie had ever had up to that time. That year, 1956, has been on my mind ever since I left Sioux Falls in 1958. The events of that football year turned the community upside down and put Augie into contention as a big power on the field. Wait till you read what I wrote. It was worth a book to my way of thinking. It needs to be edited and some I need to do some more research before it is published. I brought it along to check some facts with Ken Kessinger, the only coach I had here that is still living. I'll get the story to you so you can read it."

THE BITS AND PIECES WERE COMING BACK.

Frank Bredeson • Norma Halverson Brewer • Evelyn Brandsgaard Bridenstine • Denny Brook • Helen Brooks • Richard Brook • Beverly Brown • Keith Brown • Lois Brown • Norm Evelyn Fredricks Nancy Billy Brown • Miles Browne • Vern Broughton • Don Bruce • Phillip Bruns • Ralph Bruxvoort • Darlene Hoefert Buckley • Mary Ann Bue • Gloria Tracy Bultena • Daryl Bunde • Larry Bunde • Bob Len Tim Burhenn • Karol Scott Burke • Carolyn Burns • Joyse Tyler Buse • Barbara Graff Butts • Don Butts • George Alice Art Myrtle Irwin Helen Meek Mildred Jurgenson Lester Esther Mofle Freese • Fred Fern Grindy Gary Freese • Art Agnes Fred Sonny Dorothy Irene Freese • Fred Butler Robert Bott Barbara Jean Bott Duane Fines David Roger Butler Alyce Butler • Dale Holly Butler • Larry Buus • Joyce Byllesby • Stan Cadwell • Linda Doris Pelley Cain • Mary Lou Calkins • Shirley Callies • Betty Brewer Campbell • Dorene Campbell • Lavon Canter • Fern Chamberlain • Mavis Larson Carl • Lloyd Fern Lane Doris Bob Postma Floyd Helen Ward Glen Charolette Wesda Betty Merlynne Knock Bonnie Wyndal Conklin Lawrence Alice Robert Shirley Bibeau Chambers • Carrie Lane Ed Homer Doris Mae Rose Faye Nickolas Reiter III Roger John Judith Young Carol Earl Kidd Jr. Ella Douglas Fenstermaker Victor Kathy Ludwigs Carlson • Don Carlson • Dorothy Carlson • Karen Carlson • Barbara Chapman • Mary Cheney • Charles Chilson • Roger Christensen • Sally Bob Ronald Christianson • Gerald Christopherson • Chris Christopolis • Eva Christopulos • Don Clancy • Myrtis Clark • Ronnie Clark • Richard Clawson • Frederick Clements • Jeanette Butts Clercx • Orvil Coates • Earl Colgan Jr • John Colwell • Lorraine Hayes Sybil Hayes Irene Schurman Windy Bonnie Chambers Conklin • Darlene Conklin • Wyndal Conklin • Kathleen Rea Conradi • Larry Converse • Gene Cowan • Jacquin Cowman • Lenore Crampton • Jerry Crump • Barbara Karen Cummings • Bonnie Curl • Xenia Custer • Bob Czermak • Dorothy Fredricks Vern Gene David Paulette Ruby Landon Swensen Teresa David Stellingwerf Roxanne David Jacobsen Phillip Tammy Crystal Bartling Troy Deneice Keith Daggett • Katherine Daggett Steve Stephenie G.C. Dawn Peters • Ken Shirley Donald Debra Keith Daggett • David Lee Verne Paulette Smith Eric Amy Gayl Daggett • Ruby Daggett Landon Deana Swanson • Teresa Daggett David Tony Amber Sadie Allan Stellingwerf

continued on page 58

Roxanne Daggett David Tammy Geneva Jacobsen • Phillip Deneice
DeMent Daggett • Mike Elden Dahl • Gladys Dahl • Wayne Dahl •
Janet Dale • Delores Danielson • Richard Dargen • Tom Darr • James
Davidson • Jane Davis • Mary Ann Davis • Delores Dawley • Leonard
DeBeer • Dave Daniel David Dwain Willard Dorothy Joanne Swenson
Dedrick • Dale Delzer • Charles Decker • Lois Jennie DePew • Leah
Derscheid • George Carolyn DeShazer • Ethel Detjen • Gayle Dietz •
Dale Dobson • Buell Donaldson • Joy Donaldson • Tom Jack Donley
• Gypsy Douglas • Beverly Dresen • Charlotte Kavanagh Dreyer •
Lorraine Drummond • Joyce Duff • Florence Dumke • Barbara Dunn
• John Dal Egan • C. Dallas Egan • Douglas Egan • Albert Stephen
Mark Jan Egger • Luanne Eggers • Clair Eichinger • Robert Eichhorn
• Shirley Eichhorn • John Eich • Joel Eide • Ardis Eide • Don Ed Eide
• Paul Eischen • Jim Eitrheim • Jack Ellott • Paul Eldridge • Kay
Torkelson Elmstrand • Mary Elkanger • Robert Jim Elmen • Madalyn
Endahl • Carrol Engebretson • Edward Engebretson • Beverly Engel •
Dick Ray Beulah Desanutels Dorothy Hansen Ruth Songstad Ellen
Stephenson Engles • Joyce Lane Norman Sherron Norma Karen Floyd
Ruth Enstrom • Donna Entenman • Dick Erickson • Darrell Charles
Bill Don Erickson • Barbara Erickson • Frances Erickson • Fern Nessan
Erickson • John Duff Erickson • Sandra Espe • Loren Espeland • Jon
Falgren • Arlo Feiock • George Fendrich • Joseph Fenstermacher •
Marleen Finck • Jeanne Findley • Ron Fisher • Norman Flisrand •
Duane Floren • Henrietta Rose Floren • Keith Floren • Evelyn Fodness
• Bernell Fonder • Dean Forbord • Clarence Lily Ron Marlene Carolyn
Foss • Mike Sally Foss • Fielda Frahm • Sharon Frank • William Penn
Angeline Susan Charles Reason Cora Ellen Mae Roberts George Peter
James Orion Nancy Mary Berens Fredricks • Charles Grace Charles
'Oliver' Lois William 'Bill' LeRoy 'Roy' Frank George Elmer Della Etta
Hazel Dean Fredricks • Frank Velva Totman Grace Powderly Katherine
Hiett Harold Jeanne Hudson Fredricks • Katherine Fredricks Charlene
Rae Fredricks • John Grace Fredricks Carol Edward Patricia Dianne
Kenneth Powderly • Granville Jeanne Fredricks Dorothy Marjorie
Linda Brenda Hudson • Harold Iona Barnes Larry Lonnie Sandra
Kathy Fredricks • Elmer Ruby Lane Norma Dorothy Daggett Norman
Charles June Brandt Dick James Nancy Reuter Frank Fredricks

continued on page 78

58

5
Augustana 1951

The four years at Washington High School had proved to be a very positive experience in my life. I had acquired a great deal of confidence in myself and because of my athletic ability, a type of status that had encouraged me to project myself positively.

After my mother died in 1944, I felt totally alone. I had loved my mother and she had been a great companion to me. After she died, my personality changed. I became very guarded in my personal relationships. I felt I had been betrayed by my mother's death and I wasn't going to open myself up to disappointment again. I didn't want to get close to anyone again.

A new sense of worth developed in me. Life had been cruel, but I must go on. I began to feel and know that I was the only hope for maintaining myself and succeeding in high school and life. I began to realize that I had to chart my course myself. There was no one else to do this for me. I was in command. I was now the captain of my soul.

The second year of Coach Burns tenure at Washington High School, was a resounding triumph in the league. Almost all of our games had been won handily and the team had won the Eastern South Dakota championship for the first time in many years. It had been a great year for both the school and the community. The Heartland was happy at our success. Everybody loves a winner, and we were winners. Because of this success, all of the colleges were recruiting the players and wooing us with college football scholarships.

In the bitter cold of a January winter, mid-year graduates Bob Walton and I traveled to the State College where we were to be interviewed as part of the recruitment ritual of the mid-west colleges. We were to see the coaches, the campus, check out the atmosphere for playing there, and decide whether to make a career move that would affect our direction in life. The coaches didn't convince us that we would like the campus or the athletic program. Neither Bob nor I had been impressed. On the long ride back to Sioux Falls in Bob's car, we decided to decline the invitation to go to the State College. The problem of supporting myself at college worried me but I knew that Sioux Falls would offer more opportunity for jobs than either the State or the University towns that I had been beckoned to attend.

I chose Augie. I knew that Augie's football program has some problems, but I felt that I my presence there could turn it around and make Augie a winner. I had a great deal of confidence in myself and I felt I could fix anything by sheer determination. It was a relaxed campus and I felt that Augustana would be where I could get the best education. The campus was small, less than half the present size. The center of the campus, for me, was

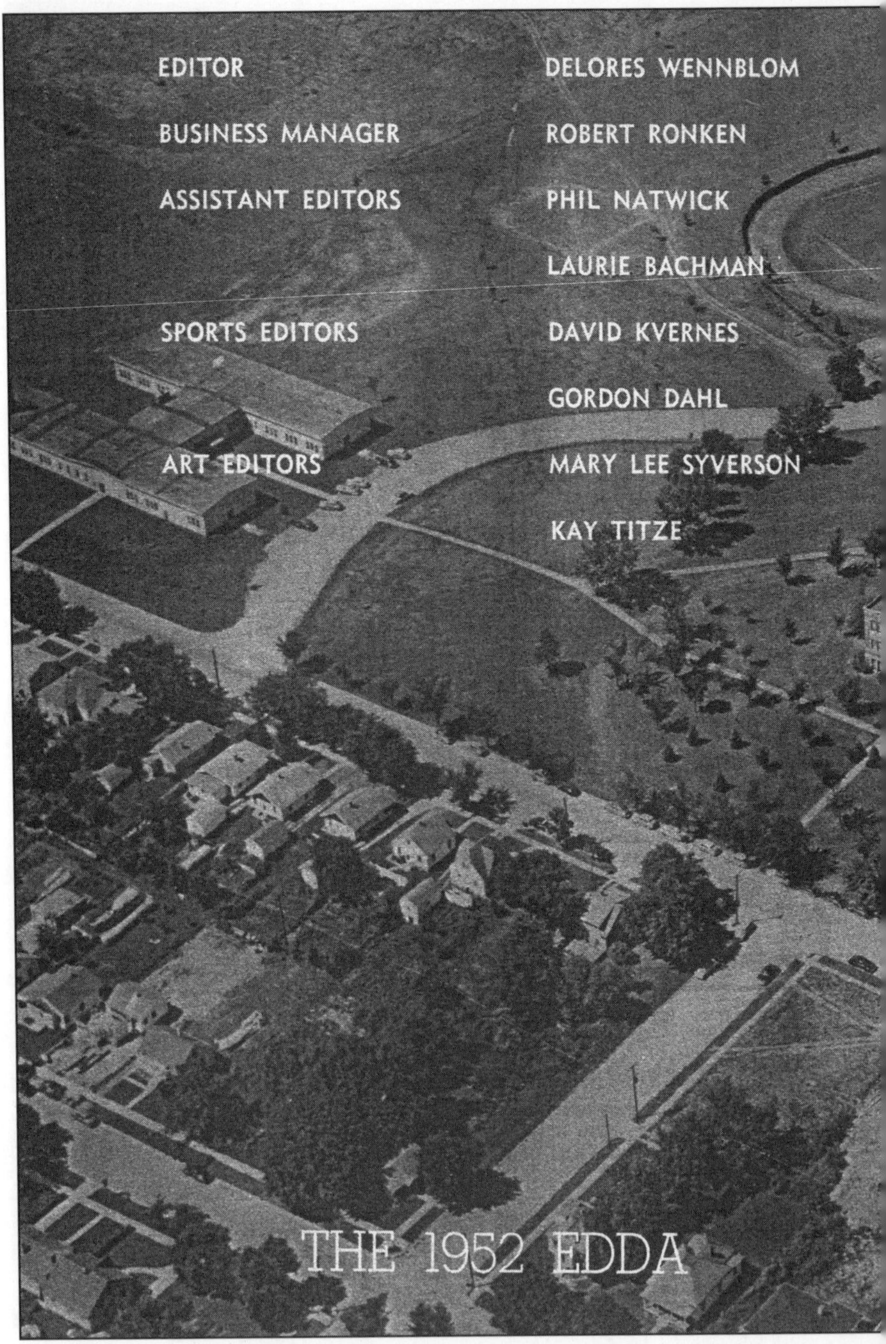

EDITOR   DELORES WENNBLOM

BUSINESS MANAGER   ROBERT RONKEN

ASSISTANT EDITORS   PHIL NATWICK

                        LAURIE BACHMAN

SPORTS EDITORS   DAVID KVERNES

                        GORDON DAHL

ART EDITORS   MARY LEE SYVERSON

                        KAY TITZE

THE 1952 EDDA

In 1952 Augustana College had about five-hundred students and the campus was concentrated along Summit Avenue and Twenty-Eighth Street. After WWII, many G.I.s returned to Augie and to provide classrooms for this increased student enroll-

AUGUSTANA COLLEGE

ment, a number of wooden barracks had been moved onto the Augie campus from the Army Air Base north of town.

61

the Gym/Huddle complex. The campus post office was in the basement as well as the popular meeting place—the 'Huddle'. Classes were held in 'Old Main', the Administration Building, and to the south of the Ad building, the Science and Arts building. The science building was a WW II wooden barracks that had been moved to the campus from the Army Base. Now, after forty-five years it had outlived its usefulness in and in 2000 it was finally torn down. A tribute to the history of the Midwest, the Center for Western Studies Building, is to be built on the site. In 1950, Tuve Hall, the dorm for the women, had been constructed. Barney was the cook at the cafeteria in another set of wooden barracks to the west of the Gym. A little over five hundred students were attending classes, and the professors were well thought of in the community.

"Fred, you register for classes next week." the voice on the phone informed me. It was the coach.

"How do I do that, coach? What do I have to do?"

"Show up on Monday, at the gymnasium. There'll be a packet of information in the mail tomorrow, complete what you can, then bring it to me at registration time Monday."

"Do I have to pay anything? I don't have any money right now."

"No, that's all been taken care of. Just show up, sign up for a English class, a social science class, maybe a German class, one religion class, and P.E. That'll give you twelve credits. Think you can handle that?"

"What's this religion class I have to take?"

"It's required. It's pretty simple. You will be able to handle it. See me Monday and I'll help you."

Registration at Augie cost about $200 in February of 1951. My scholarship would take care of that but I had to buy my books. Registration was exciting. The gym was full of new faces, lines, and confusion to me. I felt better when I saw some old buddies while standing in line. Many of the classes the coach had suggested I take were full so I had to take alternatives. The registration was accomplished in short time. I was now in college. I was inaugurated into the world of higher learning, the first attempt of anyone in my family to try this. It was history being made for my family and I felt I must not disappoint them. I had to prove my worth to them and the world.

I had taken three years of business classes and woodworking in high school. I liked numbers, organization, and challenges. An informal inventory that was given to me by the counselor at WHS, Mr. Beck, had indicated that I should make use of my number skills in college. I was good in math and at bookkeeping but I felt that I wanted to take a break from bookkeeping classes for now.

I signed up for two English classes—Composition and Literature—and two U. S. History classes. They were on Monday, Wednesday, and Friday—twelve units. My religion class was on Tuesday and Thursday, in the morning,—two more units, and I got a unit credit for spring football practice. I wasn't sure what a 'hour' meant in college but in high school a hour went by fast. What could be difficult about this? It sounded so simple. What do I do the rest of the time?

With bold resolve I tackled the classes in college with vigor and dedication.

It wasn't long before I discovered that college was very different from high school.

Augie life—1951

In addition to the responsibility of classes and study the college life offered a bold new venture into socializing on a scale quite different from high school. 'Fraternities' were at Augie and I was approached by a couple. They wanted *me* to join them. I was in demand. I was being courted by people that wanted me in their organization. That was a big change for me. The new contacts with many at the school led me into many new friendships. Now I felt I was somebody. New friends, exciting friends were everywhere. In high school I didn't date. I never had enough money to take a girl out and go to the places everyone talked about. I took a girl to a movie once and the entire night turned out to be a nightmare for me. I didn't feel comfortable so I avoided the situation by not going out until I entered college.

But now, in college I discovered the opposite sex.

....

Bits and Pieces: A family was expected after marriage occurred. Everything was learned 'firsthand' with on-the-job training. You took what you got. There was no talk of abortions or vasectomies and for that matter, sex was not discussed by either partner.

It seems that any sex discussed while I was growing up was from the pulp magazines and this sex was of the "kinky", perverse kind that left a repulsive stigma about intimacy. The Bible didn't approve of this approach to sex. Neither did it approve of sex outside of marriage. Without any preventative approach of pregnancy, the young married male and female could only hope that God would be only a little generous in his granting of fertility in the family. In our family he was overly generous.

I was eighteen. I didn't consider myself a dumb city hick although I lacked worldly experience with women. I had very little experience with sex in my short life. In high school I had kept pretty much to myself socially. My

63

mother had been a strong influence in my early life and when she had died I had felt betrayed. Betrayed by God. I remember when she had died, I was only eleven years old, I couldn't understand why she was gone. People kept telling me that God had taken her away. It was his plan they said. I didn't understand that and I felt betrayed. That attitude kept me from putting myself into another relationship where I would be vulnerable to the loss of a woman's love and understanding.

In high school I kept myself busy with activities like football, track, chorus, studying as well as working at the Sport Bowl, the ice house, and Wilson's freight dock. Idle hands are a devils workshop my aunt always said. Homework in the evenings as well as on weekends had kept me at home and out of the fast track of dating. Until I was a senior I didn't have a car to run around in. I felt that I needed a car to take a girl out on a date. I had a date once when I was a freshman. We had walked downtown to see a movie but the experience embarrassed me. The night was very awkward for me and I didn't enjoy it. 'Never again' I vowed. At least not until I could do it right. Not having a car had put a crimp in my social life I felt. However after I got my brother's car to use when I became a senior, I still didn't date. I forget what my excuse for not having dates on Saturday night was then.

I had to, however, prepare myself for the opportunity to 'make out' if the situation arose. I had glanced at the *Sunshine and Health* magazine at the bookstand at tenth and Phillips and one of my buddies confidentially told me that rubbers, called condoms now, could be purchased at the popcorn stand that stood outside of Shrivers Department Store on Eleventh Street. He had bought a pack of them there and he affirmed it by taking out his billfold and showing it to me. The tell-tell protruding round ring in his leather billfold revealed that the rubber had been in the billfold for a long time. No matter if he hadn't used one, he had it in case the opportunity arose. Ask Petersen at the popcorn stand for a pack he told me.

The consequences of unprotected sex, as it is called now, was well known to every boy in town. All of us had seen the movie advertisements posted on the Hollywood Theater front billboards showing the gross photos of the consequences of wild parties, unrestrained and unprotected sex. Once a year the shocking pictures of women with the venereal diseases of syphilis and gonorrhea were prominently displayed for this annual movie. I had never seen the actual movies they advertised but many of my friends had seen them. Their graphic descriptions scared the h... out of me. I was repulsed by this type of activity. I vowed that these types of girls would never lure me into their trap, whatever that was. The message was loud and clear—stay away from those types of girls.

The pangs of youth, however, kept stirring in me.

The chance of getting a disease was not the only concern of unprotected sex to most of the boys I knew. The chance of getting a girl pregnant had been pointed out to us very vividly by our health education teacher, Mr. Nelson.

"No man wants to marry one of 'those girls' that let every one make love to them," he told us as he gazed out of the window in a slight trance. I had always wondered about what Mr. Nelson had been thinking of as he spoke those words? Who were 'those girls'? Had I every met one of them? I wondered.

The health class was cut and dry. It had no sex movies to point out these specific pitfalls of life so the Hollywood productions were the closest thing to a educational sex movie that we knew of. I was told that the movies pointed out the gross consequences of 'sewing our oats' with ladies of the night. I knew right then that there would be no visits to the Francis' Rooms. I had heard of these 'rooms' located on Phillips Avenue over a bar. I had heard of these rooms and the whores who occupied them from numerous boys at school. I was embarrassed with the thought of them. I hated to walk down the side of the street where they were.

The thoughts of sex persisted until I felt that it was imperative that I get a 'rubber' just in case. I had to protect myself in case too great a temptation presented itself. If I didn't have the strength to resist these temptations, I needed some protection. This decision wasn't arrived at without a lot of careful thought. It was a forbidden subject to approach anyone with in the family. Sex was not a subject for discussion.

I knew that condoms were sold in drugstores but it was hard to build up the courage to find out. I couldn't just go to the drug store clerk and ask him for some. He would know what I wanted to do with them. I couldn't do that. It was too embarrassing. Also some body else in the store might hear him and look at me. I couldn't have that happen either. Nobody must know. The pressure to get some rubbers became unbearable. Finally I decided to get some at the popcorn stand. It was outside and I could ask him for them, get them, and be gone before the clerk had realized that I was there. Smart thinking I thought. And if anyone came up to the stand before I actually got them in my hand, I could ask for some popcorn to make it seem that I had made a mistake and had only come for popcorn. This had all been well thought out and timed down to the split second. The pressure to do this was immense. I became more determined to do it. I knew I had to do it. I had to be prepared.

Augie classes

I entered Augustana in the Spring of 1951, I was ready to settle down and soak up the knowledge of the world. Almost immediately I became distracted by the social life of the campus. The girls at the college were different than the ones that I had known in high school. They seemed more sophisticated. They came from all over the midwest. They had a wide range of backgrounds and that gave much more interest and spark to our conversations. I felt like I had matured overnight. The college had a lot of activities on the campus that didn't require the use of a car and that took a lot of pressure off of me. I was looking at the world in a whole new perspective now. The whirlwind life of classes, study, and socializing all came together into one all consuming activity of expression for my long awaited 'gusto for life'.

I couldn't wait to get to Augie in the morning. There was always something going on at the campus. One day as I arrived for classes I noticed a group of students watching two guys engaged in an activity. A sharp CRACK rung out. I approached to find that a couple of students—Art Huseboe and Dick Skrondal were demonstrating the use of a twenty-foot long bull whip. As they swung the bull whip a deafening CRACK again rung out. Great fun. A week later I attended a Augie/State basketball game at the coliseum. I had never gone to games at Washington High School. It was a thrilling game and Augie won. After the game pandemonium broke out. State had been robbed. Sometime during the game, some of the Augie students had 'relieved' the State cheerleaders of their mascot—the State bell. Weeks later Augie gave it back, but not before State 'ate crow'.

School was not all fun though. It proved to be harder schedule for me than I first thought. It wasn't so much that the classes were harder, it just became evident that I couldn't organize myself as well as I should have. I hadn't learned to discipline myself to study as was needed in college. I had too much freedom. It was difficult to 'hit the books' as hard as I should have. My grades were fair, but not as good as I would have liked.

As a child I always welcomed the chance to go to church. It was a fabulously exciting and organized play school for me where toys and activities that weren't to be found at home were made available to me. The church helped quell much of the aggression that had developed in me in the presence of the many rival siblings of the family. Survival is taught and learned early around the playgrounds of life in a working class neighborhood. One learned to establish himself fast or he was run over by the larger ones. You learned your niche in life fast.

I found myself rebelling against my religion classes. I felt miserable in the class. It seemed that everyone around me was so much smarter than me. It seemed that they knew everything the professor was talking about. It was all new to me. Had I bitten off too much? Maybe I wasn't ready for college. Maybe I was wasn't smart enough to do the job. I had never studied the bible like many of my classmates had. I felt at a great disadvantage. I rebelled at the thought of succeeding in this class. Doubt, indecision crept over me.

That made me even madder. The Christianity class was my worst effort and it showed in my grades.

As I approached the teenage years and after my mother's death, I stopped attending church. The church had ceased to be a part of my life. Or so I thought. Questions of 'life' and 'the path to travel' continually plagued me and made my life sometimes extremely confusing. My mother had been taken by God, so I was told. 'It was for the best,' as God had a greater need for her than I did. Why? I couldn't understand this. There were eight children in the family that now had no mother to love or guide them. Children who needed their mother. Why was God's need more important than ours? It didn't make sense. The answers weren't satisfying to me. I had to now find my way alone, so I thought.

More and more my analysis of the rituals and arguments that produced many of these faithful, produced a faith of a different type in me. Confidence in myself and my direction grew stronger the more I rejected the formalized pursuit of faith. Their faith had given me more faith in myself and my outlook on life. I grew to realize that it was the outlook of the individual that really mattered. If you felt good about yourself, that would produce faith and success. The external manifestations of clothing and hair style were not the only criteria for well-being.

Apparently the formalized approach by these people that had sometimes badgered me about their religion had succeeded, but not as they had envisioned or desired.

I had rejected their formal rituals. I could formulate arguments for my behavior and then justify them myself. That was not what the formalists wanted, but it satisfied and guided me. I had finally arrived at my personal state of faith. This was to be my direction for life. And it worked for me.

Faith in myself became the first step to success. All other things would follow.

The days lengthened. Then Spring football began. I was back in my 'element'. I felt at home with the likes of Chub Reynolds, Darrell and Chuck Erickson, Bob Walton, Dick Merrill, Jim Wylie, Charles Kemmerling—all from Washington High School. The total number of players out, however, was very small. I had been used to fifty to sixty players at WHS, and Augie had fewer than thirty practicing this spring.

Spring football practice proved to be less of a challenge than I would have liked it to be. There was very little competition in my position as a lineman. During this short time of Spring Practice I became painfully aware of Augustana College's problems in the North Central Conference. Augie's philosophy associated with athletics needed improvement. At the high school winning was expected. This college was not committed to success in athletics. Although Augie had many talented players like Little All American Dennis Erie, there just were not enough personnel to compete in the conference adequately.

Luckily the Spring practice ended without completely dampening my spirit. I sensed that Augie could overcome these adversities and prove that we could win.

Summer of 1951

Summer was near. The Spring session at Augie ended and a more pressing problem began to occupy my mind. I needed money to live on. The choice for employment was not all that great in the Mid-west in the early 1950s. At last I found a summer job that paid one dollar an hour. I took a job as a "gandy dancer" laborer for the Great Northern Railroad. It was hot, hard physical work that entailed aligning the steel rails that the train ran on, by use of brute force. A crew of six or eight men was needed for this task. Their job would consist of sticking a six foot iron rod under the rails and in unison they would pull up on the bar and move the rails ever so little until the tracks were straight. The job was within my capabilities but it quickly became evident that I would never make it my life profession. In addition to straightening the rails, the rock that surrounded the rails on the railbed had to be tamped under the rails and ties until it was solid. This was very tedious work and without a great deal of satisfying individual challenge. Day after day, the bus would take the crew of men out to a railroad that needed to be aligned and the procedure would be repeated all day throughout the summer. It was a good workout for the young kids like me and it provided enough money to live on and a little to save for the next semester.

The hour lunch time break offered me a relief from the monotony of the work. I read books that had been introduced to me the previous semester at Augie but had been unable to find the time to finish. Without a book to read one lunch time, I picked up a magazine that was on the bus and started paging through it. Finally I settled on a article about football that struck me as interesting. I started reading it.

The story line of the article captured my interest immediately. I could not put it down. I couldn't believe it. The story was so true to my own life. Almost word for word. I read on with feverishly. It couldn't be. Somebody else had been reading my thoughts. I was astounded at how close the story was to my situation.

The gist of the article told about a football team that had been dragged through the mud in their conference year after year and continually beaten by the other teams of the league. I read it avidly without putting it down. The article was so close to Augie's situation I felt someone at Augie must have written it. But no, it was in a national magazine so it couldn't have been Augie. It sure looked like it. The story concluded with the team winning the 'big game' against the powerhouse of the league. The exuberant spirit and attitude of the underdog school had won the game. The story really moved me and I swore under my breath that was going to be the outcome of Augie's football team the next year. Perseverance, desire, attitude, and team work was all that was needed to fulfill this desire.

Lessons on the 1951 gridiron

In September the football season began. It became obvious that Augustana football would be at a great disadvantage due to its lack of players. The team consisted of mainly of former Washington High School football players. They were young, immature and inexperienced. A very bad combination. The players were eager and dedicated, but there were not enough of them. The realities of life were becoming painfully clear to the young idealists.

In the first football game of the Fall of 1951, we lost to Gustavus Adolphus, eventual champion of the Minnesota Conference, in its opener by a score of 33 to 2. Former Augie Football Coach and legend player "Lefty" Olson who had a hand in scheduling the games said we should start off with the tougher opponents like Gustavus Adolphus in order to see what kind of 'stuff' we were made of. The trouble with this philosophy was that Gussie was too much for our league and their rejects from the University of Minnesota crippled or put out of commission too many of the Augie players before the season really got under way. We paid dearly for that lesson.

Despite our loss and several injuries, the next week we beat Wayne Teachers, 39 to 20. Maybe there was some hope for Augie after all. The next challenge was North Dakota State. North Dakota State, had been the acknowledged doormat of the conference for a number of years. After a hard fought battle, Augie won by a score of 12 to 0. Win we did but it was not very impressive. Lurking ahead was the real test.

Even thought talented WHS players like Bob Walton, Darrell and Charles Erickson, Chuck Reynolds, and Dick Merrill had attended Augie that year just to give Augie the personnel that they needed to win, it was not enough. The next week the roof fell in as the well coached South Dakota State beat Augie unmercifully 58 to 7. Every one of their sixty plus players were thrown into the game as the slaughter continued down to the final gun. This loss was extremely humiliating for the Augie Eleven. We fought hard but there were not enough of us. The other teams were too well coached and they outnumbered Augie players by two and three to one.

The next week, not to be outdone, South Dakota University tried to duplicate the SD State score but fell short by four points 54 to 7. They gave us no mercy and the numbers of injured players for Augie increased as the game wore on.

The following week Morningside College also trounced Augie 25 to 0 with Iowa Teachers outdoing all other conference teams 67 to 7 the following week.

The only relief from complete humiliation came in the final game which was won by Augie over it opponent, Northern Teachers, 40 to 0.

Our only conference win had been over North Dakota State. The dream that I had hoped would come true that Fall had faded by the fourth game against South Dakota State. It had been a devastatingly humiliating year for the team from Augustana.

There was no story-book ending for the team that year.

....

Weatherwax Clothing

The month after the football season ended, I was presented with a opportunity that gave me a totally new outlook on life. I got a part-time job at the Weatherwax Clothing Store. The store, situated at 128 Phillips Avenue, had been started by Frank, Sr., but his son, Frank Jr., was running the operation now. Mr. Weatherwax was a important person around Sioux Falls. Important and rich by my standard. I had passed his home that stood at the corner of Third Avenue and Twenty-first Street many times on my way to McKennan Park as a child. The house had a orange tile roof that was very impressive to me and reminded me of a Mediterranean home.

The Weatherwax store was well known in the region for its high quality men's clothing line. Our family never shopped at the store, however, due to its high prices. It represented high status to us. Many of the downtown stores except Penney's, Wards, Sears, and the ten-cents stores were too expensive for our family. Having had little money to spend, I never ventured out of my families shopping territory. The clothes that I bought at Penney's were basic denims and flannel shirts. I seldom 'dressed up' as I had no clothes to dress up in.

Ironically, while in grade school, I went on a 'white shirt' dressing kick for a while. I wore a white shirt and a tie of my fathers' every day for a while. This was completely in contradiction to my former habits. In my Eighth-grade class photo I was the only kid wearing a tie and white shirt. I borrowed a jacket and dress pants when I attended the grade school graduation. For high school graduation I wore a hand-me-down blue pin stripped suit that my brother-in-law had given to me because he had out-grown it. The pants seat was a little worn but I was thankful to have them. When I entered Augie it was the only suit that I had. That is why this job at Weatherwax Clothing Store, when I was nineteen, in college, and still very impressionable became

Phillips Avenue in Sioux Falls was an exciting place to be in 1965.

a important experience to me. My wardrobe was about to be improved drastically.

The shelves of Weatherwax presented to me a completely new world—the world of fine clothes and fashion. I had never seen a Harris Tweed top coat or Van Heusen shirts. I had never been able to afford much beyond basic clothing up to this point in my life. As a child, my father bought me one pair of shoes a year. They were high topped 'Farmer's clod hoppers' and cost about one dollar and a half. I had coveted having a pair of 'tennis shoes' but I never owned a pair of them until I was in college. Nike and other famous name brand 'Jock" tennis shoes were not invented yet. Denim pants, cheap sox that wore out fast, a couple of shirts, and a coat in the winter was about all my father could afford. If the shoes wore out before the year was up, tough. I remember many a time I walked around with my shoe soles 'flapping' because they came loose. I had to walk like a duck due to them being loose. A visit to the shoe repair shop cost money. Most of the summer I went around bare footed. The first purchase at Weatherwax by me was a pair of Imperial Florsheim shoes that cost Fifteen dollars. Fifteen dollars was a fortune to me, but I was impressed with the pair of Florsheim that Coach Burns wore and I was determined to have a pair.

One of my duties at the store was to attach price tags to the clothing before they were put onto the main floor. I had never seen so much variety of clothing in my life. I looked at my own wardrobe and realized how poorly I was dressed. The salesmen at the store wore white shirts and ties, and a suit. I wore my best slacks and whatever shirt I could find. After a few days I felt pathetic and I knew I had to have better clothes to wear. I felt the desire to look better, dress better, and try to be on a par with my classmates at Augustana. I began looking more closely at the variety and quality of the clothes I handled. I began comparing prices. I needed clothes but I knew my dollar a hour salary wasn't going to buy everything I wanted. I had to be cautious, and thrifty.

I tried on jackets that came in. They felt good. Almost every color accentuated my large body and blond hair. I felt stunning in these new clothes. It wasn't long before I acquired an entirely new wardrobe. I felt sharp for the first time in my life. I developed a entirely new type of image for myself in the new clothes.

At Christmas time Mr. Weatherwax asked me to drive him and his wife to Florida for their annual vacation. For me this was a really big deal! I had never been beyond Kansas City or Minneapolis and this trip was much further. My horizon was expanding. We left after Christmas in Mr. Weatherwax's Lincoln town car. It was awesome. We ate at the best restaurants and slept in the best hotels. It was first-class all the way. A snowstorm in South Dakota had delayed our departure so the agenda had to be changed. After driving them to Shreveport, Louisiana, I was to fly back to Sioux Falls in order to return to my classes at Augie. My first airplane ride, albeit in a two-engine airplane was a highlight of my young career.

....

I continued working at Weatherwax's during the summer. The job was easy and didn't require much brain power. In fact, working in the basement was very boring for me and lunch was very much looked forward to. Every noon hour, however, presented a challenge. What could I find to do that was exciting? After using only five or ten minutes to eat the sandwiches that I had, I had fifty minutes to pass before returning to work again. At first it was hard figuring out what to do but eventually I developed a habit of taking a book to work to read. After a while even that got boring and staying at my workplace during lunch was too convenient for the salesmen at Weatherwax to interrupt me and ask me to run errands for them. I had to try somewhere else to read. But where?

I had to get out of the basement so I decided to take a walk. I walked south along Phillips Avenue. After ten minutes of walking I found myself at the corner of Fourteenth and Phillips. Lyons Park was across the street. Crossing the intersection, I glanced up and looked at the old civil war cannon and a Union soldier with a rifle that stood as sentinels to the beautiful park. They had been given to the city years before and put in full view of the main boulevard to remind us of the sacrifice others had given to make our country what it is today.

As I climbed the slight hill into the park I started looking for a bench that was under a shade tree. I spotted one far back in the park. As I got nearer to the bench I suddenly became aware of another person, a girl, seated across from the bench I was going to sit at. I changed my mind and ambled over to her bench and sat down. The girl was beautiful. She was smartly dressed in a light print dress that was very transparent and flimsy. Very nice I thought. Wonder why she is here? Maybe its her lunch hour also. Wonder where she works. As I had approached the bench she had glanced up at me and gave me a big smile. I smiled back and slowly opened my book to a page and looked over to her.

"Hello", I said. She responded with a nod of her head as she glanced into my eyes.

"What are you reading?" she asked me.

"Oh, nothing, just something I just picked up to find out if I wanted to read it. Nothing important, just something to kill the lunch hour," I answered.

The conversation ceased and out of the corner of my eye I sensed her staring at the tree across from them. I sensed she wasn't really looking at it.

"Nice day," I blurted out suddenly.

"Yes. So you're on your noon break?"

"Yeah. What about you?"

"No. I'm just enjoying the park on my way home." She glanced toward me. "My name is Veronica. What's yours?"

Wow, what a beauty. I now closed the book sensing that the ice had been broken and that she wanted to talk. I couldn't concentrate on the book now anyway. The sweet smell of her perfume was driving me crazy and I felt nervous and agitated.

The weather topic had been explored so I tried to think of other approaches to a conversation.

"What do you do?" I asked.

"I'm a student at the University. Working during the summer so I can go back in the Fall. How about you? What do you do?"

"I go to Augie but I need to work this summer also. At Weatherwax Clothing downtown.' I volunteered.

"Oh, Augie, that's a good school. Do you know Don Jenson there? I met him once."

"No. I don't think I do. Name doesn't sound familiar."

"No, how about Johnny Jones? He was at a party I went to once. Do you live in town?"

After a half hour of petty, nonchalant conversation, I started growing restless because I knew that I had to return to work shortly. By now neither of us wanted to end the conversation and the relationship.

"How about meeting me for a beer after work tonight?" she suddenly asked. "We could meet at the Red Rooster and have a beer there."

I didn't drink beer or anything alcoholic, but I didn't want her to know it. And I didn't go into places like the Red Rooster. This question made me feel very uncomfortable but I wanted to see her again.

I had to think quickly. "No, I may have to work later tonight at the store. I don't know when I'll be finished for sure."

"Why don't you come to my apartment for a while and we'll talk before I have to go to work, say around 7 o'clock? Could you be there then?" she asked.

Her apartment? Alone with her? My head was reeling with thoughts of passion and romance. "All right, I should be able to be there." I said calmly. She gave me the directions to her apartment. It wasn't but a block from the park.

The afternoon was spent marking a shipment of suits and shirts that had come in at noon. I then carried them to the main floor of the store and put them on the shelves. My mind wasn't on my work and a couple of times I was reminded to put the suits in the right rack. I kept thinking of what I was going to say and do at Veronica's apartment that night. I had lied to her about working late and I couldn't wait to get out of the store at the 5 o'clock closing.

I didn't walk home that afternoon but I took the bus instead. I wanted to get home fast and get ready to go see Veronica. By the time six thirty had rolled around I had finished bathing and shaving. I slapped on my after-shave lotion. Man I felt and smelled sexy.

It was hot outside and I worried about sweating too much. I started walking down the street at too fast a pace considering the weather. Take it easy I told myself. No need to hurry, she'll still be there when you get there.

Although it was actually only a twenty minutes walk, it seemed like an hour. I walked up the front cement steps of what looked like a apartment complex on Fourteenth Street between First and Second Avenue. As I approached the two story apartment house I remembered she had directed me to stay to the left of the front porch and go to the back to a side entrance. The door and two large windows on the alley side of the building looked out onto the porch. I took a deep breath, waited a second, and then I knocked.

"Hi, come on in." she said as she opened the door.

She was dressed in a pair of shorts that left nothing to my imagination. She looked great. She was a knockout for beauty. The door led into a large room that had a kitchen nook and stove to the rear of it. The room had a sofa, coffee table and a couple of chairs in the center set on a large throw rug. A dresser with a large full length mirror beside it was to the west wall.

"Do you want a beer?" she asked as she snapped the cap off of the one she was holding. She was looking at me with half closed eyes that didn't betray the fact that she had already had a few beers.

"No. Do you have a coke?"

"I think so." She opened the refrigerator and peered in and pulled out a bottle of coke and opened it.

"Here's to you." She toasted and she lifted the beer to her lips and drank.

The muslin curtains on the east windows filtered the harsh light out of the room and made it glow ever so soft. It was warm in the room and I felt overdressed and warm. The cool coke felt good going down my throat and drinking it gave me a good reason to pause in the forced conversation about the weather. We made small talk of no consequences. Finally she went to get another beer and as she returned from the kitchen she intentionally brushed my body. That was all we needed to look at each other and embrace. We kissed. Man, what a long, prolonged kiss she gave me. It didn't stop and I didn't want it to stop.

Suddenly to my amazement she looked at the clock on the wall and shrieked. "I've got to get to work. I didn't realize how late it was. You've got to go, right now."

"Go? What do you mean, go?" I said.

"Oh, I'm sorry. My boss called me and told me I had to come in early tonight. I've got to go. You've got to leave."

I knew I had been 'had'. She didn't like me for some reason. Maybe I was too naive. I felt angry, outraged and embarrassed as I left her apartment. I felt like a nerd also but I waved good-by as I left. As I neared the front of the porch, I was suddenly aware of a group of my buddies across the street engaged in a bit of horseplay and shouting. Catching sight of me, they all of a sudden stopped talking and looked at me without saying anything. I nodded recognition, waved a short, curt wave with my hand as I walked down the steps and began walking toward town.

Working with me at the Weatherwax store was an older man who frequented the bars at night. Ever since I began working there he had tried to impress me with his knowledge of the night life of the town. Suddenly I decided to ask him about Veronica. "Hey Palmer, do you know a gal named Veronica? She works at a place called the Red Rooster."

"Veronica? Yeah, sure. A real doll. Seen her a lot of times. All of my buddies have tried to get a date with her but she keeps refusing them. Heard she got kicked out of the University. Too much partying and there was talk of her being too easy with the boys. Some type of scandal happened but I don't know any details. Why do you ask?"

"Oh, no reason. I just heard the name," I lied.

"She's one hot dame. Would like to...you know what."

At work the following Monday one of my buddies approached me and after talking a little while he asked me point blank how I had gotten a date with Veronica. Apparently every one them had tried and failed to date her at the Red Rooster where she worked. They had found out that she had been kicked out of the University the last semester for engaging in too much extracurricular activity with some boys at a Frat party, and she had moved to Sioux Falls. Nobody had been able to get her out on a date. How did I do it?

I didn't answer. I slowly walked away leaving him there with all of his unanswered questions. My buddies never did find out from me what had went on inside that apartment that night but I knew that I had gained a higher degree of awe and respect from them as I had walked out of Veronica's apartment that day.

....

I was extremely discouraged with the 1951 football season. It had been a disaster.

After a year of classes at Augie I decided I was on the wrong track. My individual initiative and curiosity were extremely important factors that had not been taken in account adequately in the inventory tests but through insight and maturity I personally discovered a new direction to go. I re-channeled my effort into the field of science when I discovered the excitement that the biology classes gave me. The business classes were no longer stimulating and biology gave me an entirely different outlook to life. I started looking around for another school that could fulfill my curiosity. At the end of the summer I decided to transfer to Kansas University.

In 1956 most of the Augustana College campus was still on the north part of the campus.

Norman Elaine Klinghagen Nancy Carol Jo Bruce Fredricks • James
Douglas Jeffery James Joseph Charles Fredricks • Frank Kathryn Nye
Susan Steven Sherry Fredricks • Darold 'Dick' Peggy Jones Kim Meyer
Karol Gallucci Fredricks • Ralph Swanson Nancy Fredricks LuAnn
Ralph Art Reuter • Dr. Sven David Tom Kristi Karen Susan Froiland •
Lloyd Frost • Russell Gaffney • Ole Garvick • James Gednalske • Joyce
Geiver • Charles Geyer • Don Gerlach • Marv Gerlach • Charles
Gerlinger • Jerry Germany • Deon Gerry • Ronald Giedd • Curt
Gifford • Lois Gilbertson • Edna Gilbertson • Margaret Gildemeister •
Wayne Gildseth • Janell Gill • Barbara Gilman • Donald Genther •
Celeste Glanzer • Florence Glanzer • Paul Glanzer • William Goebel •
Irene Goldammer • Marlo Goodroad • Harris Gorder • Barbara Graf •
Don Grebin • Hazel Green • Jerrould Green • Lois Greenough • Ron
Greenslate • Dick Bonnie Gregerson • James Gremmels • Lenita Prouty
Groos • Doris Groth • Joan Keep Gueffroy • Richard Gunther •
Georgia Gulbrandson • Greta Gulbranson • Harold Gunderson •
Marcia Gunderson • Richard Gunderson • Richard Gunnarson • Carl
Guthals • LaVerne Haas • Sally Haas • Carolyn Haga • Virginia
Gregorson Haggar • Leonard Haggin • Wesley Ken Halbritter • Jim
Halpin • Bruce Halverson • Shirley Hammarley • Mary Lou Bud
Donahoe Connie Emery Filmore Barbara Greno Hanger • Elinor
Hanson Hansen • Marlys Hanson • Thomas Hanson • Lois Becker
Hanson • Pauline Hanson • JoAnn Hanson • Winetta Hanson • Gary
Sandra Fredricks Kathy Jo Hanson • Barbara Hanvelt • Constance
Haney • Joan Hardy • Bruce Haroldson • Marilyn Caldwell Harmer •
Wayne Harris • Verner Hartmann • Bill Harvey • Lee Bob Blance Falor
Evelyn Pelley Harvey • Clara Milt Harvey • Dick Ted Harriman • Mary
Hasson • Marianne Hauge • Harriet Hegstrum Hauge • Sandy Haugen
• Roger Haugo • Yvonne Haugse • Len Haugse • Marian Slaman
Haugsted • Veloy Hawkey • Jack Hawkins • Dorothy Heckt • Julie
Luella Hegstrum • John Heidal • Glennis Heikes • Paul Heine • Donna
Helgeson • Kayle Helgerson • Berverly Allard Hendrix • Ruth Herbst
• Marilyn Hermanson • Leslie Hernes • Joel Hernes • Virginia
Herrboldt • Robert Hersrud •Eugene Hervig • Carol Hewlett • Charles
Hibbison • Dennis Higgason • Edith Hill • Ordelle Hill • Val Rhea
Hill • Rick Hiller • Dean Hinders • Jill Hines • Norm Hines

continued on page 106

6
The Spring of '56

"Hey, Elmer, what do you think of the news?" a man down the bar asked. It wasn't exactly a bar, but a place to get a good, cool beer on a hot day—Pinards Drugs. Pinards, a two-story wooden building, stood on the corner of Eighteenth Street and Minnesota Avenue. It was an 'old fashioned' drug store, well patronized, with a counter immediately inside the front door, and a drug counter in the back section of connected rooms where sundry goods could be purchased by the customer. At the front counter—'bar'—lemon-lime phosphates, cherry-cokes, ice-cream concoctions as well as beer could be purchased. On the wall, behind the counter, there were large mirrors. The atmosphere inside was peaceful, and cool. A few small round tables no larger than the size of postage stamps (or so they seemed) could be found in the back of the drug store. The wire backed chairs weren't the most comfortable to sit in, but what the hell, it was better than sitting out in the sun.

"What news? I haven't heard anything new lately," Elmer replied after swallowing a mouthful of cool beer. He then wiped his mouth with the back of his shirt sleeve and sighed.

"I thought you had a boy playing football at Augie?" the man asked.

"I do. He played last season after getting back from the army." Elmer answered as his eyes adjusted to the subdued light inside of the building. Outside the bright sun beat down on the cement and it was hot.

"Last year was a disaster." the man said. "Man they lost it. Wasn't all their fault though. The rest of the league was too strong for Augie, and Augie didn't have enough personnel to spell the first string. They had a few good veteran players, but they weren't enough." The man sounded very knowledgeable and Elmer listened with his head down, looking at the bar before him.

"Yeah, my son wasn't too happy with the last year," Elmer finally said. "He didn't play very much."

"Why was that?" another person asked. "I've been to some of the games, and whenever he's in the game he looks like a damn good player. I don't understand that. He was a good player under Burns when he played at Washington High School. Remember that first year Burns came to Washington High?"

"Came from Yankton, didn't he?" the first man asked. "In '48 or '49?"

"Yeah, in '49. He was too good for that size of a school. Came here in 1949 and took over. The teams hadn't been doing very good when he got here and his first year was so-so, but he really took off after his second year. After his first few games he put it together and started winning. Ended it being the best in the league, but he started off slow."

Bob Bittner, Dick Fredricks and Jim Howlin take out time for a photo in the old Viking Stadium.

Fourteen Augie linemen of the 1955 team line up for a photo.

"He needed to get his offense established with the new players on the team, and after he changed some personnel he began to click." the man said.

"Yeah, I remember his second year. It was really a barn-burner. Was beat by only Rapid City. If I remember right, he started a 30 game win streak that year." the second one offered.

"NO, it was a 37 game win streak he had. Finally lost to a team out in Wyoming. He told me that he and the team took a plane to the game, but they forgot to take any oxygen tanks along for use by the players. The higher altitude did them in." the first man said.

Elmer sipped his beer and listened. The two men seemed to be enjoying themselves as they discussed football.

"Washington High is the biggest high school in the state. They have over 2,500 students and they should never lose at anything considering all of the talent they have to choose from," the first one said.

"Unless you get out-coached," the second one quickly said. "I've seen a lot of teams win just because of the coach's abilities. I've seen that too many times to count. Best talented team can't win if they are out-coached. That's why football is so exciting. On any given day, almost any team can get beaten if they don't perform as expected."

"All they need is a bad day."

Turning to Elmer, the man continued, "I wondered what had happened to your son the past few years. You say he was in the army?"

"Yes, he went to Augie to play after he got out of high school but he left Augie after playing his freshman year there. He was disgusted with the football program at Augie so he transferred to Kansas University. He couldn't play varsity there when he transferred because of eligibility rules, but he played on the scrimmage squad until he quit to go to work. At the end of the year he was drafted into the army."

"So that's what happened to him. What did he do in the army? Did he go to Korea?"

"No, he was sent to Germany and did something in a office. He did play one season on the army team over there. Said everyone was a pro on the team, or a semi-pro. Very rough he said." He took another sip from the mug of beer. He smiled to himself. Seemed like old times to Elmer. He liked it when people he didn't know recognized him, or found out he had a son on the team. Good feeling being recognized for his son's achievements. Those were good days at Washington High School. Then he went to Augie and the pats on the back stopped when their team lost continually.

"The army? I've heard that some of their teams at the bases are better than the pros. That's why he looked so good last year. The times I saw him play last year he was all over the field. He has really matured."

"And he was ready to make a big contribution to Augie when he came back from the army last year and although its a smaller school than Kansas University, he decided to return to Augie because he thought he could make a difference. He would have last year but he had a little run-in with the coach."

"A run-in with the coach?"

"Yes. The coach asked him his opinion one day about the offense they were using, and he told the coach what he thought. It was too slow, and the quarterback tipped off the plays to the defense in too many ways. He suggested some changes but the coach took it as an insult, got mad as hell and didn't talk to him, or ask him his opinion again. He just kept him sitting on the bench."

"So that's why he didn't play very much. I talked to him a few times and I found out he was really knowledgeable—and smart about football. I thought he was better than the guy he played behind, and now that explains it. Well, he won't have to sit on the bench this year."

"What? Why?" Elmer suddenly asked as he swung his head to look at the man talking.

"That's the news."

"What's the news?"

"Bob Burns is going to Augie. Its in the newspaper. Headlines. He's accepted the coaching job at the school. He's leaving Washington High School."

"How will that change my son's chances of playing?"

"Hell, he was with Burns at Washington the first two years he came into the league and he knows Dick is a hell of a good player. Burns will play him, don't you worry."

"Well, he got a job up in Montana this summer, and he'll be home by the end of summer, ready to play." Elmer finished his beer and left.

On the road to Montana

The Buick's engine was humming beautifully as it headed west along Highway 16. The sun was high in the sky and it was hot. The two of us in the front seat sat looking ahead at the road that stretched out before us.

Although surrounded by the trappings of civilization, Bob in the drivers seat felt the spirit of high adventure, much like pioneers that had settled the area a hundred years ago, as the town we had just left quickly passed from our thoughts. We felt like we were explorers heading into the sunset.

For the next month we would be sleeping out under the stars, in the wild open spaces. We would be challenging nature, living with the hardships of the prairie in the comfort of a modern automobile. This was as close to the pristine, rugged individualist's life of the past that we would ever get. It was exhilarating thinking about it. And it was under control.

"Man that sun is hot." Bob said as he rolled down the window to let in air. "Hot flowing air is better than no air." he said as he wiped his brow with his hand.

"Better get used to it. It'll be hot until we reach Mitchell," I said slowly, but decisively. I glanced toward the slim but solidly built man next to me. "We'll be facing it for about an hour and a half then we'll head north. Should be cooler by then. Would you rather be riding on that truck that Dick has to be on?" I asked.

"Hell no. He can have it. This is hot enough. I'm just happy to get out of town. Man, I was getting sick of waiting. For a while there, I thought it was never going to happen."

I gave no comment. The driver kept his eyes on the road and glanced down occasionally at the speedometer, keeping it at a steady fifty-five. A steady thump, thump, thump was heard as the tires hit the asphalt dividers on the cement road. It was annoying at first but after a while it beat a rhythm that was mesmerizing. Comfort in an uncertain world.

My thoughts kept coming, bits and pieces. Everything we owned, which was very little, was in the green '49 Buick. Everything. Sleeping bags were piled on the floor behind us. In the back seat lay three hand bags. Each contained a couple of pairs of shorts, socks, and a few shirts. We wore a pair of army fatigue pants, and an army shirt. Our boots were army issue. They had seen a lot of travel, and they were cut off at the tops to make them easier to get on. Brogans, they were now called.

Bob glanced over at me. My huge muscled arms bulged from underneath the army shirt that was obviously too small for me. I had cut the arms off of the shirt but it was still too tight, too small for my large frame.

That was it. Life was simple. We wanted it that way. For the next month or so it would remain that way. Everything I had was in the Buick. We would live out of it, eat out of it and sleep in it at times. We could survive anything nature could offer us—the wind, the rain, the heat, or any other thing that would come along. Nothing was going to bother or defeat us.

I squinted, trying to block out the glare from the cement road ahead, wishing I had some sunglasses. I glanced over at Bob. He was wearing his sunglasses. The dark glass concealed his eyes and gave him a extremely macho look. With his free hand, he pulled his straw hat down a little to block out some of the direct rays of the sun. He glanced up into the rear-view mirror, checking himself, and checking his persona.

"Sunglasses sure help a lot against this glare." Bob said half in conversation and in a boasting tone.

He had glasses, I didn't. The sunglasses he wore were dark black and hid his eyes completely. Air Force issue. Mystique. That's what it did for him. "Mystique. That's what the girlies want." he suddenly said. "Mystique, and a good time."

"What? What did you say? I can't hear you. The open window over here makes too damn much noise and unless you talk louder, I can't hear you."

"Mystique." he repeated louder. "The girls like a man with mystique. These glasses get them every time."

"Yeah, yeah...well, I'll have to get some. They really impress the girls." Why does he have to wear that damn straw-hat in the car when he's wearing sunglasses? Why in hell does he have to do that?, I thought as I tried to hide my irritation at the nature of the conversation.

The sun continued to beat down on us. It was hot. The Buick continued down the road at a steady fifty-five miles per hour. The road continued on straight path before us—up slight hills, then down through slight valleys, but ever on straight ahead.

"Look, you can see the road ten miles ahead its so damn flat out here." Bob said. "Never seems to stop. Just goes on and on."

"No it doesn't." I shot back at him defensively. "There are hills and mountains before you get to the West Coast. The Rockies are out there." I offered. "You ever been to the West Coast, Bob?"

"No. Went to Idaho once. Didn't like it though."

"Not the same as California. After I got back from the Army last summer, me and a couple of guys took off for California—Santa Monica. That's by L.A. Man it was a great trip."

"Those are the guys you do gymnastics—tumbling—with, aren't they?"

"Yeah, we fooled around with it," I suddenly said with exuberance in my voice. "Started doing tumbling with them after I got mustered out of the Army last year. Taught gymnastics for the city recreation department during the last school year. Did it a couple nights a week for the elementary school kids. Lots of fun. Didn't pay much though. There's no money in it. Nothing pays anything around here. Work like hell and don't get anything ahead. Man, I can't wait to get out and find a place where I can make some money. California looked good. A lot of jobs are out there, not like it is around here...and good paying ones too. 'Specially if you have a college education. The whole country's screaming for teachers and college grads out there."

"How are the women out there? Better than here?"

"Hell everybody looks better out there. They dress better, smell better, make more money out there. If you can't land a job out there you're a real loser. Lawrence Welk broadcasts from out there. He's from South Dakota you know. He sure made it big out there. We went down to where he plays, along

Dale Fellows (top) and Dick Fredricks, along with Bill Bubbers practice gymnastics on the grass at Drake Springs on a Sunday afternoon.

the ocean in a big dance hall. His T.V. show is broadcast from there. Everybody out in California lives better than we do. There's more money floating around in Santa Monica than we have in the entire state. Just aren't any jobs or money around here."

"Yeah, but money isn't everything." Bob protested.

Suddenly I felt betrayed. I wanted Bob to agree that a life did exist out in California, and that it would be worth trying to get. "Did you ever try buying a car without it?" I shot back sarcastically. "Or clothes? or a house? Say what you want to but you need to get some money or everyone will always crap on you."

"Well, we've got a job now." Bob said and he reached over and slapped me on the leg, trying to change the direction of the conversation that had gotten too serious. God he hated serious conversations that had no ending to them.

"A job? Yeah, big deal. At a buck a hour. If we work. Nobody ever really said how much we will work."

"Peterson said it would last for five or six weeks. They worked steady down in Iowa. Heard it from a couple of guys I know was there. No over-time, but steady work, day in and day out."

"Except for now. Now they have to travel to North Dakota and Montana or they're finished. They don't get paid to travel. That'll cost them. That's why we have a job now. Most of them don't want to go to Montana and work for a measly buck a hour. And we'd better be back in six weeks or I'll be out of there. We need to be back for the beginning of football practice. Nothing's going to stop me from being back here for that, especially this job."

"We'll be back for that. What the hell, we weren't doing anything any-way. It's better than sitting around on our butts, and we can get in shape while we're getting paid. Don't get all riled up about getting back. Enjoy what we have while we can. We'd be rotting in town for the next month if we had-n't taken the job."

Suddenly I was furious. "That's you're problem." I shouted over the noise of the car, the tires, the air coming in the open windows, "You are satisfied too easily. If you had to hustle like I've had to, you'd think differently." and as quickly as I had exploded with anger, I checked myself and shut up. Damn it, I thought to myself, I'd better learn to shut up before we get in a fight. Hell, I have to live with him for the next month or so and we'd better get along or it will be a miserable time. I've got to shut my mouth and let a lot slide by. I've to stop getting mad about little things.

Damn I shouldn't have got him started, Bob thought. I forgot he had a short fuse. Never know what will set him off. Damn I hope he settles down on this trip, I don't know how much I can stand of this attitude. He really gets worked up over nothing. I've got to watch myself.

An attempt was made to change the subject. "Wonder what time Merrill will start for North Dakota?" Bob asked. "The trucks with the equipment on weren't in town when we left. Be hot as hell if they leave before it gets dark." but he noticed I wasn't listening as I appeared deep in thought. I had picked up a road map from the seat and was looking at it.

The sun and the heat took its toll on the two of us and we settled down to watch the road and the countryside as it passed rapidly by. Both of us wanted to be alone with our thoughts for a while. The hum of the motor helped us drift into a state that offered this.

What a scene to paint, Bob thought. "Fred, this is magnificent. Look at that sun."

"Yeah, hot as hell."

"No, no, look at its color. Brilliant yellow, and look at what it does to the countryside. It gives it life. It gives it purpose."

"Oh, that's right, you're a artist, a painter. You look differently at everything. To me it's bright, and its hot."

"It's more than that, its beyond just hot and mean," Bob said. "It's what makes us able to be us, it is the wonderment of mankind. He's worshiped it for thousands of years. It's mesmerized and intrigued him ever since time began for man. It is more than just a big yellow thing up there in the sky. It is...magnificent. I only wish I had my paints here right now to paint it."

"What do you do, scenes?"

"I like to paint scenes, I like to paint buildings, I like to paint still life, but most of all I like to paint the human body. That is the ultimate. The body."

"You ever painted women? Nude women?" I asked as I glanced over at Bob.

"When I was overseas, in Italy. I did a few women. It was great. Fred, you were stationed in Germany, right?" I nodded after Bob spoke. "What did you do?"

I thought a second, then spoke. "Yes, I was there in '53 and '54. A year and a half. Took my basic training at Camp Chaffee, Arkansas, then specialized in the 105 Howitzer. Our group was then assigned to Germany. I really liked it over there. Great duty. It gave me a chance to do a lot of traveling around Europe, and read a lot. One day the captain asked me if I wanted to play football for the army. I was bored with the office and I said 'yes'. That cut me out of a corporal stripe but I didn't care."

"You played football for the Army? How'd you do?" Bob asked.

"It was good duty. I had a great time even though I didn't play all of the time. Lots of talent in the army. We had semi-pros on the team, a lot of college players, and a number of kids just out of high school. Unfortunately the coach was a real bastard. He wasn't happy with his duty, the time off they gave for his coaching, and I think he was having trouble with his wife. He didn't put much time in it or give it much thought. If it hadn't been for a couple of other good coaches, non-coms, on the team, he would have killed us. One guy in particular set up the offense and defense before he was rotated to the States, and the Lieutenant never changed the team or any of the offense the rest of the year. He just didn't give a damn. The poor guys on the first-string never got relieved once they started the game, no matter what the score was. We had a lot of talent and I learned a lot just watching the guys play."

"I can't wait to get back to playing football." Bob said anxiously.

....

Augustana opened up many vistas for me after graduation from Washington High School. College was as different as night and day to me. A completely new routine had to be learned. I was on my own, making my own decisions in an entirely different sense from the high school days. I loved the challenge it presented. I took two history classes from professor Solberg. They were fascinating. His insight into the history of the world astounded me. I was so unaware that history could be so stimulating. I never knew so many things had happened over the course of mankind. European history was the professor's strongest interest and as he talked about the European empires—the Huns, Franks, Roman Empire, etc., etc., I became extremely anxious to see the world—especially Europe. But how? Not on the resources I had. To make things worse, it seemed like everyone else I met in college had been out of the United States, or dreamed of going just as I was doing. The thought of traveling became all-consuming and it frustrated me to no end that I couldn't afford to do it.

After the disastrous 1951 football season at Augie, I transferred to Kansas University for my sophomore year of study. I was broke after paying the $200 for tuition and fees. so I got a job at a medical fraternity washing dishes. I was paid a dollar a day and given my meals. I took a full load of courses—German, Biology, a history course, and a English class. The challenge at K. U. was so great that by the end of the semester I had lost thirty pounds. In May I received a letter from my draft board in Sioux Falls that informed me that at the end of the year I was to be drafted into the Army. The United States was still engaged in the Korean War and my number came up. I left Kansas University at the end of the Spring semester. After boot-training in

Paris

Germany

Rome

Arkansas, I was sent to Germany to serve out the remainder of my time. I was finally going to Europe.

I arrived in Germany a week before Thanksgiving, 1953. Luck was with me. The two years of college prep gave me an edge in being assigned to a desk job. Most of my buddies that I had taken 105-Howitzer training with were going to spend their time outside in the cold on field maneuvers. I took a typing test, passed it, and was assigned a desk job in Kaiserslautern. I welcomed the challenge of change. The United States was in the Cold War with Russia and we were almost on the front line in Germany.

I was inside behind a desk, and I had a full-time pass for after-hours. My German language skills were put to the test right away as we had Germans working on the base. For the first time in my life I felt wonderful about everything. I had regular meals, I had money, $110 a month to spend and my job demanded very little time. I immediately took advantage of my ability to travel and I went to Munich, Heidelberg, and Cologne the first three weekends I was in Germany. Later I went to Frankfurt, Paris, Nice, London, Rome, Florence and many, many other smaller cities. I continually took advantage of my free time by traveling. It was a time of great exploration for me.

....

We settled down now, watching the road and the countryside as the miles added up on the speedometer. Fifty miles...Sixty miles. The golden brown wheat fields zipped by. The corn in the fields was over two feet tall now. Both events were soothing to me as I looked out the window. Looked to me like a good crop was to had again this year.

"Mitchell ahead." Bob finally said. "Want to get something to eat?"

"No, lets wait a while."

I checked the gas gauge. Should have enough to get to Huron. Bob picked up the map laying on the seat.

"Hey, Fred, let's keep on 16 for twenty miles more. This map shows Highway 281 ahead that is a straight shot to the north. We don't have to go through Huron, keep on straight ahead."

"O.K. We'll take 281 north up ahead. At least the sun will be out of my eyes."

"Might as well drive on through the night until we get tired." I said. "Should be getting cooler in a little while. That'll make it better and keep the car cooler. Tires will last longer when they're cooler. We'll drive all night if we feel all right."

I'd been watching the road, mesmerized by the rhythmic bump, bump, bump of the road dividers on the tires. I had been thinking of California, and the trip last summer. It had been a great trip. Everywhere along the coast had seemed so refreshing, and cool. Here, it was always hot, hot, hot. There was no change in the weather all summer. Only an occasional rain to cool things off. Once it became hot, it was hot. And in the winter, once it became cold, it was cold. Hot and cold. Cold and hot. It never let up. Now Santa Monica was different. It had been cool during the nights, and only slightly warm during the days. And if it got too hot, the ocean was there to take a dip in. The place was clean, cool, and bustling with activity. When it was hot here, everybody died and did nothing. That heat really sapped the strength out of you, and makes you feel like hell. Oh yes, you worked, but you wished you didn't have to. That heat; it was almost criminal to go out in it at times. But in California. That was different. At least along the Coast.

Bob stopped when we turned north and I took over driving.

Aberdeen

The sky in the west was changing into a yawning chasm of darkness. The mood of the prairie was changing also. Driving at dawn or dusk has a certain beauty about it. The transition from light to dark or dark to light offers mood changes that can be equaled at no other time of the day.

"Aberdeen ahead." I yelled to be heard over the sound of the engine and the air flowing into the car from the open windows. Bob jerked upright in his seat.

"God, don't do that." Bob said. "I was in another world".

"Let's eat a bite and rest for a while. I need to stretch my legs."

The big, four-door Buick rolled to a halt in the dirt parking lot in front of a cafe. There was a yellowish light shining from a pole to the left of the parking lot.

"You sure you want to stop here?" I asked. "Looks like something out of a Erskine Caldwell novel."

"Maybe we should find a better looking cafe."

"It'll be O.K." I assured him. "I need to stop and go to the john. Besides its the only place I can see around here anyway. Not much of a choice but I'm too bushed to wait until Aberdeen. Let's get coffee here anyway then stop in Aberdeen for some good food."

Stepping out of the car we both stretched and looked around. The cafe looked a little better now that we were out of the car. A couple of tables were occupied and a car pulled up as we began strolling toward the front door. We sat down at a table next to the front windows and looked at the menu.

A young girl appeared at their table with two glasses of water, put them down before us and asked what they wanted?

"A burger." I spoke up. "and a cup of coffee."

"Want fries with it?" the waiter asked.

"Okay."

"Me too." Bob echoed.

She wrote it down and walked away. Bob watched her go, running his eyes up and down her figure. "Not bad." he said as she walked away, "looks like I gal I knew in Naples. Boy was she great, all of the time."

"Oh, that's right, you were in Naples. In the Air Force, right? How was it over there? I went through there in '54, on my way to Capri, but I didn't see anything I wanted to stay for. You just got out of the Air Force, what? a couple of months ago?"

"I wasn't right in Naples, a short distance away, at a small base where I was an M.P.—military police. Played policeman at the main gate for two years. We had it dicked there. Little duty, lots of free time, and plenty of women. I did a hell-of-a-lot of painting there. Painted almost all of the time. But you're right. Naples wasn't a place to be in unless you needed to. Yeah, two months now I've been out. I had enough of the service, but it was great while it lasted. You went to the Isle of Capri? I heard that was a great place. That island had been a famous resort since the days of the Romans."

"Yeah, great place. Went over on a boat and was going to stay one day, but stayed a week. What a place. Water everywhere. A hell of a lot different than around here. The history that place has seen. Like to go back some day for a visit. The mainland down there was the pits though, except for Pompeii. That was a great place to visit."

"You were stationed in Germany, right? What did you do?"

"Yes, '53 and '54. A year and a half. Great duty up there. Did a lot of traveling around Europe, played football for the Army, and read a lot."

"I can't wait to get back to playing football." Bob said anxiously. "Been a few years since I've played and I want to get back into it. I really like the game. Wasn't any team to play on over there. You were lucky you had a team in Germany. I've thought a lot about it and I know I can play a better game than I did the first year at college before I went into the Air Force. That was hell down at Nebraska. All they did was practice, the year around. Nobody had any fun. I'm looking forward to this year, especially now since Burns is going to coach at Augie."

"You know that first year that I went to Augie, after high school, we did-n't win a game that year. No, that's not true, we won one, at North Dakota. But everybody beat North Dakota. State and the University humiliated us. Each one tried to run the score up as high as they could. Sixty or seventy points they beat us by. Hell it was like we weren't there. Did it again last year. The bastards. If we have any chance at all this year, it'll be because Burns is coaching us. Hell, we've got almost the same team he had while we were in high school. We have the talent."

. . . .

"I'll drive." Bob said as we exited the cafe.

Looking at the sky I said. "Such a beautiful night, look at that Western sky." The sky had faded to almost a shade of pitch black but the area where the sun had went down was still slightly aglow, giving it a lingering magical feeling. It was a stupendous feeling I had as I walked to the car. A feeling of freedom. A feeling of the start toward a new beginning. Beginnings of trips had always instilled this in me. It was a high that I never grew tried of.

We continued north, following the asphalt trail that would lead to a few weeks of hard work and time to think.

The hum of the motor, the sound of the tires on the road, and the light from the headlights on the road were perfect conditions for thinking, and I felt like reflecting. I had always considered myself a dreamer, a thinker, a philosopher, although my family never seemed to recognize these qualities. At least they never spoke of it. Their lives were wrapped up in living for the moment. They never seemed to let themselves think of anything else but their own lives. Ever since I could remember, I felt detached from the rest of my family, and the other people that came into my life. I was an observer. A thinker. Detached from much of the other world.

"Hey, Bob, the town of Frederick is just ahead. Just before we cross into North Dakota. Wonder if any of my ancestors settled here? Could have just spelled the name wrong, on something. Mighty unusual name for a town. At least they, whoever they were, got some recognition in their lifetime. Having a town named for you would at least insure that somebody would remember you for a little while after you died, or moved along." Bob nodded his head at what I said, but said nothing.

The car sped into the night.

Sixty miles had passed. "Jamestown is just ahead." Bob blurted as if not believing it was his voice.

Jamestown? I thought for a second. Jamestown, that's where Louis L'Amour lived at one time. Or was he born there?. "Hey, Bob, Louis L'Amour lived here when he was a kid. Louis L'Amour... what a man." I said. "What a successful person and writer. Wow, his books are the best. Man alone against the elements. Man and nature, against all odds".

Men riding for the brand! For the brand. That's what I do. Ride for the brand. Always have. But I haven't won! Should have been a winner after high school, but I wasn't. Should have been though. I sure as hell tried. Gave it my all.

"You know, Bob, with Coach Burns at the helm again at Augustana next year, we should have one hell of a year."

I will be a winner, I said to myself as I continued to think about football. Just like L'Amour. Riding for the brand. And he wins out. Hondo, one of the greatest books ever written. A classic by any standard. Alone, against the world, but with compassion, and eventually the love he has earned. Hondo. Man against the elements. Oh how I'd like to write like him. He had to have the greatest life on earth to live like he did. He can really touch the human soul in his books. What a man.

"Yeah, it'll be interesting," Bob commented as he continued watching the road ahead.

7
Summer's End

"Who wants to drive?" I asked.

"I'll drive." Merrill offered.

"Check around. This is the last chance to see this part of the country for a long time, if ever. This is it. **It's over.**" I shouted as I walked around the Buick checking the tires and car over. "Now we can go back to play football. Next week we begin training. I'm ready."

"Man, I feel like a million bucks. This work up here in Montana has paid off. This is the best shape I've been in my life." Bob said.

"Me too," Merrill said. "I must of lost fifteen pounds of fat this summer. My pants hardly fit any more."

"You'd better throw those motley Army pants away. Better yet, burn them."

"Okay, okay, pile in. If we start now, we should be there by tomorrow sometime." I said.

Bob, Merrill, and I got into the Buick, Merrill behind the wheel. I took a last look at the grain bins we had just finished, and sighed. It was over, we were heading for Sioux Falls.

....

The Burns Factor

Augustana College's football teams had earned a reputation for being the doormat of the North Central Conference teams. They did this by losing almost every game since the mid '40s. Some years they did win one game and that one game was with North Dakota State. It was almost understood that no team except North Dakota State would lose to Augie. Augie was routinely trounced by South Dakota University and South Dakota State, Augie's traditional rivals, to the tune of a 40 to 50 point margin. This humiliation was hard to take even by Lutherans.

In Spring of 1956, Bob Burns announced acceptance of the head football coaching position and Athletic Director at Augustana. Coach Burns, at Augie? The football community was stunned. Why is he going to Augie everyone was asking? He can coach almost anywhere now that he's the most successful high school coach in the midwest.

Coach Burns had produced a football dynasty at Washington High School since his debut in 1949. The Warriors had achieved stupendous results under his rein—including a 37 game winning streak that began his first year at Washington High School. Teams challenging WHS from

Augustana College

Lloyd McKenzie

Bob Newcomb

Carl Guthals

Arlo Feiock

Bob Walton

Dick Fredericks

Vern Broughton

Paul Heine

Bill Simpson

Terry Hokenstad

Paul Rogness

Ken Richards

Jon Falgren

Phil Nelson

Football 1956

Minnesota, Iowa, Wyoming, Nebraska as well as South Dakota met defeat from the skillful coaching of Bob Burns and his capable assistant Grant Heckinlively. Their success was so overwhelming that Washington High School finally felt compelled to drop the traditional confines of their Eastern South Dakota Conference and began acting as a independent competitor without a league.

Augustana College was the doormat of the league. In the 1955 football season, Augie had won only one game.

"What's the deal? Why is Burns going to Augustana? He's a Catholic you know."

Questions kept popping up over the campus: How could the Lutherans hire him? Will he go to Chapel services like the other faculty members? Will the members of the Lutheran Church cooperate with him? How long will he stay here and coach?

Bob Burns' style of coaching and his record at WHS were legendary even to non-football enthusiasts in the area. He projected a confidence and aura that influenced everyone that met him. Everyone wanted to share in his success. Almost overnight the Augie booster club became a bee hive of activity. Every member sensed a change for the good in the community. The business community rallied behind him. Men that had never participated in Augie's activities became eager to offer financial support to make Burn's attempt at Augie football a success. The phones at the athletic department were ringing constantly. Applications in the Augie booster club doubled, then tripled. The word was out. Finally the 'underdog' was to get a new lease on life and the thought of success sent chills of delight throughout the community.

....

Augie Football—the Men—1956

A meeting was being held in the athletic office adjacent to the gymnasium: It was a bleak room, devoid of any frills. The room had a desk, a chair behind it, and two other wooden chairs. The chair behind the desk was occupied by Coach Burns, the two wooden chairs had respectively Marv Rist and Mr. Peterson sitting in them.

Burns looked at the two men and spoke. "Well, Pete, we have a hell of a job ahead of us. I just read some predictions by the press and they give us last place in the league this year. State and the University are to finish at the top of the league. Do you think we've bitten off too much?" he asked not fully expecting an answer.

"What do you mean, 'bitten off too much,' the fortyish-aged man asked. "You've got a hell of a task before you but you knew what you were getting into. Anyway, sports writers don't play the games. They have been known to be wrong."

"They've been known to be wrong, true, but not this wrong. They're all saying the same thing. There's a lot of hope for me but this year doesn't look good. I thought I knew what I was doing when I decided to come to Augie." Burns answered. "Too late now to turn back the clock. It looks bleak though. Marv and I have just been looking over the equipment and I don't have to tell you we need everything. There aren't even enough jock-straps for all the players. All of the pads are almost shot. And there's only enough good equipment for about twenty players to be fully outfitted. Shoes are in a mess, half are without cleats, helmets are scratched, dented, or without paint."

"Well, that's no problem. I can get the paint to spruce them up. Might even come up with some new color to set Augie off from the rest."

"Yeah, well, the painting of the helmets isn't going to get me any new equipment, or personnel so we can field at least one good team." Burns looked dejected at this point and slammed his fist down hard onto the top of the desk.

"Well, now wait a minute." Pete shouted. "The people around here want a good football team. You have offered to coach for the school, a school that hasn't exactly supported the team with the money needed to play in this tough league. We know you're a fighter, not a quitter. We all know that. So if you need equipment and other supplies, we should figure out a way to get the money to get the stuff."

"And personnel." Marv butted in. "How are we going to field even a half way descent team unless we get some more personnel? We need more players but the regents won't allow us any more budget. We need more men! Hell you can't play with only twenty players in this league. State and the University each have over eighty players they can draw on. We can't play on the same field with them with only twenty or twenty-five players no matter how dedicated and good they are."

"I've been thinking a lot about that," Burns said. "They expect a miracle from us but we need at least three years to build a good, solid team. It can't happen overnight. I read one of the writers give Augie a chance to take next to last in the league." he said sarcastically. "South Dakota University is to take the championship, followed by South Dakota State. Now there's a sobering thought. We play the 'U' in three weeks and then we have State to face. But there is a way to speed the process of getting experienced players for this year. We can get as many junior-college recruits as we can afford. They will have had two years of experience before finishing at the junior college and there should be quite a few willing to come to Augie. If we can find them. The few recruits we've gotten from the Junior Colleges will help but we need more men in order to survive injuries that are bound to come."

Bob Burns stood up and began pacing back and forth in his tiny office. Pete watched him then suddenly stood up himself, looked straight at Burns and said, "I know I can get some money, and the people to back you. Your decision to come to Augie is already the only topic I hear wherever I go and I know if we get a quarterback club, a boosters club, and hit a few of the businessmen at the right time, we can raise a lot of dough to get the equipment. Leave it to me, I know how to do it. I'll get started on it right away. Can I use the phone in the other room?"

Looking astonished, Burns nodded his head. Now he had them he thought. "Now we can really get going. With Pete on our team, we can't lose." he said to Marv.

Immediately all aspects of the Augustana football program were examined and re-examined by Coach Burns and his new assistant, former college team mate and coach, Marv Rist. These two capable men were very well aware that their success had to be achieved in order to salvage some dignity for the City of Sioux Falls and Augustana College whom some thought were synonymous.

With a new budget and contributions from the community, new equipment was chosen and ordered. Finally new football shoes could be offered to the returning players—at least to the first string. Varied colored helmets were painted by Sunderman in hopes of creating a new image for the team. Blocking and field practice equipment was constructed and donated by Augie fans and supporters.

"This is great," Burns said to Marv, "but we can't let the community get too high in their expectations for this year, its getting out of hand."

"Let them go. It's good for the community. We've done almost all we can humanly do for this year." Marv finally said. "All we can do now is coach the hell out of what we've got and hope for the best. Maybe we can catch a few more when school begins, like some returning servicemen. The Korean War is over and a lot of athletes went to the service a few years ago. Let's hope we can get a windfall of returnees. Heard Bob Walton and Dick Merrill are out of the service and may come back to Augie. A couple of more Junior College transfers would help, and I've been talking to two from over in Iowa."

Gradually as the summer months of preparation for the new season wound down, a new exuberant Augie spirit began emerging.

But the big question remained—could Augustana shake off its losing ways and compete with the other NCC schools in the conference? If they could get the many seasoned veteran players like Bob Walton, Ben and Bob Newcomb, Phil Nelson, Dick Fredricks, Chuck Howlin, Carl Guthels, Paul

Heine, and Jim Westby, to name a few—to play over their heads, and not get injured, they had a chance to give their opponents a season to remember.

Burns and Rist continued to actively recruit junior college transfers such as Milt Archer, Bob Weber, and Bob Wells with hopes of getting some depth to his first team. Without a little depth to his team there would be little chance of playing out the year and becoming a winner. These new recruits would help. With his usual foresight, Coach Burns began to build a team for the future, as he immediately induced a number of his former high school athletics that had contributed to his success at WHS to enroll at Augie. Although they would not be eligible to play the first year, these men could prove to be invaluable in their workouts against the varsity.

....

"How many men have we got to practice with today?" Burns asked Marv.

"Looks like we have 24 that can practice," he replied.

"Twenty-four! How can that be? We had thirty-three last Monday. What happened to the rest?"

"Too many have fallen by the wayside." Marv replied. "Six had turned in their equipment by Wednesday, remember?. Went back home. Four have injuries—ankles, bruises, small things but they can't practice."

"Six junior-college transfers were suppose to be here today," Burns said. Maybe they'll show this afternoon. This morning we'll practice on the south forty, south of the stadium. There are a lot of gopher holes down there so we'll have to be careful. Send out the grounds-keeper to check again and plug up any holes he finds. Put the injured players on the dummy bags today. At least they can hold up the dummies so the others can run plays. They can't get hurt doing that," Burns answered anxiously. Burns was staring at the floor, shaking his head. "We can't afford any more injuries. We've got to pull back on the practices and save the men for the games. I've got to at least field a complete team. We don't have even enough men to do a hard practice with. Twenty-one players! And half of them are almost useless."

"Now that's not true Bob" Ken injected into the conversation. "Everyone we have out there is doing his best with what he has. Not all are what you want in a player, but they will play as hard as they can, and produce. We've got twenty-one players, but they will all come around and do the job. With more experience, we should be able to field a good team by this Saturday."

"God, this Saturday." Burns shouted. "That soon already? Jeeze, I've been so intent on practice, I forgot it was that soon."

The phone rang. Burns picked up the receiver and held it for a second. "Can't be bad news, we have enough to last us a lifetime now. 'Hello'," he barked into the mouthpiece. Yeah, Neuser, how you doing? Yeah? OK. That's great. When? OK," and Burns hung up.

"What was that about?" Marv asked.

"That was Neuser Salem. He says he's contacted a few of his former players and told them to be here this morning to scrimmage. He figured he could help with a scrimmage, as well as help us coach to get ready for the game this Saturday."

"That sounds great. We need all the help we can get. At least we'll have enough to have a scrimmage with now."

"Yeah, at least I'll have something to talk about at the Quarterback Club meeting today at noon."

"OH, I had forgotten about the Quarterback Club meeting. That's at noon? Over at the Cottage, right?" Ken said.

"Yes," Burns answered. "We'll leave right after practice this morning, I've got a meeting with a few guys before the formal meeting. Maybe I can get some money from Harold for a camera and film to take pictures of the games."

"Yeah, that's a great idea. You did that when you were at Washington High, didn't you?"

"Yes. It helped a lot to see the players in the actual game conditions. Nobody can deny what happens or have a alibi for their mistakes that you can see in the film.

But the big question remained—could Augustana field a team for the Saturday game, shake off its losing ways and compete with the other N.C.C. schools?

Quarterback Club—September 10, 1956

A trickle of men arriving at the Cottage became a torrent of two-piece suits by noon as the ones who couldn't get off early from work arrived. The place was full by 12:03 and an extra room was set up for the late-comers. Hamburger, beans, salad, cake, and coffee was the fare set up buffet style at the side of the room. The noise level increased as the men finished eating. Eyes continually shifted from the people at the tables to the table on a small elevated platform in front of them. The mood was jovial, but all were anxious to hear about the coming football season. Would there be anything for them to cheer about? What would the great Bob Burns promise? What could he do this year at Augie? At least the reactivated football 'club' would give them a different thing to do for Monday noon lunches. Summer is the pits with no football or basketball to occupy their time. Small talk centered around the new football season while they waited for the meeting to begin.

Coach Burns finally stood up and gazed around at the crowd. He nodded his head to a number of people. He knew it was too late to back out now.

This is what they've come to see. Burns was nervous as he tapped on a glass with his fork to get their attention.

"Looks like a lynch mob," Burns quipped. Everyone laughed. "I've seen a more friendly group up at the prison than I see here today." Again laughter. "Ten minutes ago I felt like walking out and going home. I don't know what to say, I feel like a condemned man waiting for the executioner to come. And I believe that is what this football season will be like—an execution." Again a nervous laugh rippled through the crowd. Some looked at each other and shook they head slowly in affirmation. "If you remember, Augie won only one—one—game last year. I hope to at least tie that record, I'm trying to schedule Sioux Falls College instead of playing the University." Laughter. "This year is going to be a great challenge. When I made the decision to take over the reins at Augie last Spring, I felt that all that was needed here was some new equipment and a few good plays, and I would be able to live with anything that would come. I really didn't know how bad it could be. But now I know. If anybody else gets injured in practice, we won't have enough personnel to field a team. It really looks bleak for the first game we'll be playing this Saturday. If you want to see a blood bath, just come out this Saturday."

"What a bunch of bull. I'm going to cry." someone commented to the person beside him. "I've seen them practice. They're in great shape for this game." The person next to him smiled.

"That's Burns."

Burns kept looking out at the crowd, focusing on individuals for a while then moving on to look at another person. He was good at this. He caught and held their attention. He actually made them begin feeling sorry for him. He knew he had them where he wanted them now. Pity. Pity was what he needed now. "Don't get your hopes too high for this year. It's going to be a dog fight, all the way. I don't expect to win any games. I just hope to show up and give it our best. We'll be lucky to field enough players to make a team. Our only hope is that we don't get too many injuries at the start of the season."

Now he had them going, Burns thought. Pity. And compassion. That's it. Get pity and compassion and they'll show up for the games, if only to see my ass kicked all over hell.

Burns continued. "There are some bright spots. The cheerleaders look great this year." (laughter) Burns continued, "At least I've got a few seasoned veteran players in Bob Walton, Ben and Bob Newcomb, Phil Nelson, Dick Fredricks, Chuck Howlin, Carl Guthels, Paul Heine, and Jim Westby to name a few. The team will have to be built around them. Expect them to be playing a lot. They will have to even with this new two-platoon system we have now. They're good men. But not enough." Some had heard this before, but now he hoped he could get some sponsors for some extra money to get more players. "Most of the men are still in fairly good health. No big injuries. Hell, who am I kidding? I don't have even enough players to field a good scrimmage for the first team in practice. We're just not deep in players like our opponents. Man, State had over ninety out at practice every day. The University has over eighty available to play. Talk about depth. I would like to have their rejects for my team." Slight laughter. "We have at the present twenty-two good players without injuries. Twenty-two." A murmur went through the crowd. Many hung their heads down and shook them slowly. Burns paused and took another drink of water. "And five or six more that can hold bags to run some plays against. I can't even scrimmage the rest of the week. If any other players gets hurt, I may have to suit up and go in." Laughter. "But the ones I have are all veteran players," he was dead serious now, "and they know how to play football. Linemen—Simpson, Fredricks, Newcomb, Richards—now there's a big guy -, Hokenstead, they will give their opponents a reason for remembering them. Quarterback, now that's a tough one. I've been putting Phil Nelson in that spot, but I don't know how long he can last, he's got bad knees. That's why I can't let him play end as he had been doing." Burns looked around. Best decision I made was getting him out of the end position. He's a born quarterback. Wonder why he wasn't put there before now? "Got a couple of scat backs, Chuck Howlin and Arlo Feiock, who'll do great if we can get them around the end of the line. They'll be great because with their size, they'd better run like hell just to keep out of the grasps of the other team's linemen." A huge roar of laughter went up. Coach Burns began fidgeting with the knife and fork on the table before him. "I did get some lucky breaks so far. I've been recruiting some former players from Washington High School. Bob Walton for one. He should be great at end. He just got out of the Air Force, in fact he got an early discharge to get here for the football season. Many that I've got signed for Augie, like Glenn Sellevold...Pat Smith...Don Renner, won't be eligible until next year. That's what I have to look forward to. Next year. This year will be a building year. Got a couple of Junior College transfers, Milt Archer and Bob Weber. They'll help, but will it be enough? Unfortunately, when any of them become injured, there is nobody to put in their place. Everyone had better pray that nobody gets hurt.

"I've devised a few good plays for the game this week against Wayne State. Last year Augie lost by a score of 0 to 0. At least we didn't get trounced." Laughter. "Thank god the game is here at home so we'll be fresh. But the second game against North Dakota State is up in North Dakota and that's not going to be to our advantage. All I can ask is that you support Augie this Saturday and hope that we can end the season with at least one win. It could be a hell of a season to watch and I'll try to show some good football if some more players I've recruited get here before the season begins. If I can get at least ten more players, I could finish the season, but it'll be a tough row to hoe."

The crowd walked out of the restaurant in a very subdued mood. 'It would be worth going to the game just to see Burns get knocked on his butt,' one of the men commented.

Jean Hintze Lamb • Dale Hintze • Mary Ellen Hinzman • Rudolph
Hoffman • Roger Hoier • Dorothy Hoogestratt • Gladys Hooestratt •
Evon Hoover • Ike Hoover • Gayle Hoover • Terry Hokenstad • Soffie
Hoines • Dick Hopewell • Bill Horeis • Merle Becker Horton • Robert
Houser • Richard Howes • James Charles Howlin • Robert Janet Huhn
• Art Huseboe • Gerald Ihrke • Wilma Inglis • James Diana Basel Irish
• Ileen Wageman Irvin • Richard Irvine • Monte Irwin • Myrna Irwin
• Cecil Myrtle Freese Loren Dolly Irwin • Joan Jacobson • Loreli James
• Barbara Jameson • Ronald Jamtgaard • Richard Janisch • Edward
Jansen • Charles Jarratt • Betty Rahn Jasper • Patsy Jenkins • Dick
Jensen • Natalie Jensen • Chuck Jerde • Carole Johlfs • Audrey Johnson
• Beverly Johnson • Carolyn Johnson • Dave Johnson • Delores
Johnson • Diane Johnson • Donald Johnson • Fred Johnson • George
Johnson • Helen Johnson • Leland Johnson • Lorraine Johnnson •
Marilyn Johnson • Sharon Johnson • Martha Johnston • Donald Jones
• Jacquelyn Jones • Joanne Jones • Bill Minnie Putzke Merlyn Dorothy
Bob Swavely Carol Hoover Ken Peggy Fredricks Jones • Wyman Carol
Jones Kent Hoover • Kenneth Juanita William John Katherine Jones •
Merlyn Dorothy Weisser Susan Brian Dana Erik Swanson Jones •
Robert 'Bob' Kay Jane William Theresa Alvin Leonard Lena David
Swavely • Janice Cecil Jons • Pat Jorgenson • James Josephson • Larry
Josephson • Charles Jude • Ellen Juhl • Irma Juntunen • Maureen
Kampen • Dick Kaus • Leona Kearney • Jan Keenan • Charles Jr
Kemerling • Richard Kersten • Ken Kessinger • Margaret Bonnie Dave
Kiesow • Tom Peter Jamie Kilian • Maxine Killeaney • Larry King • Eva
Kirchner • Marylyn Kirkpatrick • Kenneth Kirkvold • Joseph Klock •
Dennis Knight • Nyla Knudtson • Carol Knudson • Roxanna Kohrs •
Paul Betty Ball Kolb • Jim Kolb • Dean Koolbeck • William Kraft • Jim
Kragness • Kenneth Kramer • Paul Kranz • Herb Krause • Donald
Krenos • Addie Larson Keep Krogmann • Roger Kruse • Avis Calkins
Kruse • Carole Kvam • Eugene Lahammer • Robert Larson • Joseph
William 'Bill' Clara Beeson Albert 'Lee' Mable Ball Edna McKean
Gertrude Evans Laura 'Bill' McKean LaFollet • Albert 'Lee' Emma Lee
Shiela Shirley Moore Arlene Delight LaFollet • Boyd Landsman • John
Carrie Lintner Doris Chambers Geneva Johnson Roy Russell Ruby
Fredricks Carrie Carlson Lawrence Gerald Vance Joyce Enstrom Lane

continued on page 119

8

What happened in the fall of 1956?

NEW ENTHUSIASM IS FOUND IN NCC

Jim Burt, sports director of KELO Radio-TV,
comments on the 1956 NCC grid season.

The North Central Conference has entered many interesting and sparkling football seasons in the record book. While the past few years have been slim for a few members of the NCC, and little interest shown toward their efforts, a spark of enthusiasm and a new glow of spirit apparently has been kindled among the alumni, fans and players, as we begin the 1956 campaign.

New faces among the coaching ranks probably have been a factor in stimulating much of the desire for the keener interest.

Year after year, the North Central football loop is regarded one of the 'tough' ones in small college leagues. And this season certainly is no exception. In the past, it's been an accepted fact that any one club could beat another team on any given Saturday. Since the loop is shaping up on a more equitable basis than in recent years, this appears to be even more true. Thus, it should be a peak year for North Central football. An to forecast the one team to carry off top honors is a paramount challenge.

North Dakota U. could be considered a chief threat, but early season injuries, with a lack of depth, may reduce the Sioux chances.

South Dakota U. has one of the loop's new coaches in Ralph "Boot" Stewart, who came into a squad of veterans, including two all-conference backs. The Coyotes certainly will be a major contender.

Main competition, too, may come from Morningside, which is fortified by letterman at nearly every position.

Iowa State Teachers suffered heavy losses by graduation, but a fine crop of youngsters ranks the Panthers as the conference darkhorse.

South Dakota State will be hard-pressed to retain its championship. The Jackrabbits lost six regulars, four of them all-conference performers.

New Augustana Coach Bob Burns debuts as a college mentor and attempts to return the Vikings to former grid heights. Augie is not expected to make much of a dent this season, and it's a long climb from the lower echelon where the Vikings have been secure. Should an established determination and strong desire hold in the camp, the Oikles should shake loose under the new regime and start on the upward trail to soon rate distinct recognition.

North Dakota State has the third new coach in the conference. Les Luymes takes over the Bison reins after a winless 1955 season. Again, the Bison have been ranked last in pre-season conference ratings. Bolstered by a

Augustana Starting Line-Up

LE	LT	LG	C	RG	RT	RE
Paul Heine	Ken Richards	Dick Fredricks	Bob Newcomb	Terry Hokenstad	Carl Guthals	Bob Wal
74	78	71	55	79	75	61

QB
Phil Nelson
70

LHB
Chuck Howlin
46

RHB
Jon Falgren
47

FB
Arlo Feiock
56

VIKING ROSTER

No.	NAME	POSITION	WT	HT	CLASS	HOME TOW
41	Hopewell, Dick	B	150	5-7	So.	Sioux Falls,
46	Howlin, Chuck°°	B	160	5-9	Sr.	Grand Forks,
43	McKenzie, Lloyd	B	155	5-9	So.	Williston,
44	Rygh, Roger°°	B	165	5-8	Sr.	Roseau,
45	Newcomb, Ben°°	B	170	5-10	Sr.	Sioux Falls,
47	Falgren, Jon°	B	165	5-11	Jr.	East Grand Forks,
49	Athey, Bob	B	165	5-9	Jr.	Estherville
51	Dietz, Gayle	B	175	6-0	Jr.	Russell,
53	Berdahl, Charles	T	180	6-1	So.	Garretson,
54	Boettcher, Dick°°	C	175	5-11	Sr.	Aberdeen,
55	Newcomb, Bob°°	C	175	5-10	Sr.	Sioux Falls,
56	Feiock, Arlo°	B	175	5-11	Jr.	Aberdeen,
58	Merrill, Dick	T	180	6-0	So.	Sioux Falls,
59	Rogness, Paul°	C	185	6-0	Jr.	St. Paul,
60	Tallakson, Warren (Lee)	C	190	5-11	So.	Sisseton,
61	Walton, Bob	E	185	6-0	So.	Sioux Falls,
62	Westby, Jim	G	190	6-0	So.	Sioux Falls,
63	Archer, Milton	B	175	6-0	Jr.	Estherville
64	Ratzloff, Jim	B	185	6-1	Jr.	Windom,
65	Broughton, Vern°	E	180	5-11	Jr.	Lynd,
66	Jones, Don	E	185	6-2	Sr.	Rapid City
67	Weber, Bob	B	200	6-4	Jr.	Estherville
68	Wells, Bob	B	190	6-2	Jr.	Estherville
69	Rohwer, Tom°	G	198	6-2	Jr.	Park Rapids,
70	Nelson, Phil°°	B	195	6-1	Sr.	Minneapolis,
71	Fredricks, Dick°°	T	185	5-10	Jr.	Sioux Falls,
73	Erickson, Jerome	T	190	6-0	So.	Baltic,
74	Heine, Paul°	E	190	6-3	Sr.	Hibbing,
75	Guthals, Carl°	T	205	6-1	Jr.	Fowler
76	Berven, John°	T	205	6-1	Jr.	Mitchell
77	Rogness, Steve	T	200	6-0	So.	St. Paul,
78	Richards, Ken°	G	220	5-11	Sr.	Eveleth
79	Hokenstad, Terry°	T	200	6-2	Jr.	Crete
80	Simpson, Bill°°	T	190	6-0	Sr.	Sioux Falls

*Denotes Lettermen

Front row: Lloyd McKenzie, Arlo Feiock, Dick Merrill, Chuck Howlin, Jon Falgren, Gayle Dietz, Bob Athey, Dick Boettcher, Roger Rygh and Ben Newcomb. Second Row: Paul Rogness, Terry Hokenstad, Steve Rogness, Bill Simpson, Don Jones, Chuck Berdahl, Bob Wells, Jerry Frey and Vern Broughton. Third Row: Jim Ratzloff, Dick Fredricks, Paul Heine, Bob Weber, Lee Tallakson, Jim Westby, Carl Guthals and Bob Newcomb. Fourth row: Bob Walton, Phil Nelson, Jerome Erickson, Dick Hopewell, John Berven, Ken Richards, Leland Johnson, Tom Rohwer and Milton Archer.

109

Ken Kessinger, Bob Burns and Marv Rist plan strategy for the next game.

promising freshmen crop, there's evidence State may cause some concern before the season is over.

....

Augie Coaches: Tonight a new two-man team will be guiding the Viking varsity in their first game of the season. Both Burns and Rist have had a wealth football experience behind them and are counted on to build a ball club that will send the Vikings on the upward trail.

Burns, the former coach of Sioux Falls, Washington High, played his high school ball at Sioux City Central and later entered the University of South Dakota, where he captained the Coyotes in his senior year and was All-North Central Conference for two seasons.

Marv Rist comes to Augustana from the University of South Dakota, where he was assistant varsity coach for Harry Gamage. Rist also played college ball at USD, after graduation from Centerville High School. At USD he too became captain of the squad in his senior year and was on the all-conference team.

Freshman coach Ken Kessinger is back for his third year at Augustana. Ken, an alumnus of Augie, is counted on to mold a frosh team to fit into next year's varsity. Drills for the frosh are scheduled to begin just after registration is completed. In addition to frosh football, Ken handles the freshman basketball squad

....

Coach Burns and Coach Rist were excellent judges of football talent. This was their genius. This became clear when they decided to move Phil Nelson from his traditional position as a end to the new quarterback position.

Phil Nelson was a born leader. The players respected him. He had excellent height, over six feet tall, and strength and ability as a end, but Burns thought he would excel as a quarterback. After watching a number of workouts at this position, Burns and Rist agree he was the man for the position. This proved to be the move that sparked the teams spirit to lofty heights above and beyond that exhibited by past Augie teams.

"I wish we had two more backs to spell Roger Rygh and Chuck Howlin," Burns commented. "They are going to need some relief during the games."

"Wish they were twenty pounds heavier and four inches taller, that's my wish," Marv said and laughed.

"Hell, if they were that size they'd be playing at Nebraska or Iowa. They'll get by here. They're quick as hell, that all that counts now. Arlo Feiock and Jon Falgren look good so far. That covers the main back spots we need to worry about. We do have McKenzie and Hopewell to back them up when we need them."

"We've got a good line," Marv said as he looked at a list. "Richards, 220, Hokenstad, 200, Carl Guthals, 205, Bervin 205...that's not bad weight. Fredricks, Bob Newcomb, Simpson, Rohwer, and Westby are lighter, but they're quick, and fast. That could be the difference—quickness. The 'T' formation requires quickness and they have it." Marv kept looking at the paper. "If need be we could shift some of the other players, like Weber and Wells to tackle position, if we get in trouble."

"Okay, make a note, for now tell them to learn the linemen's position for some of the basic plays," Burns said, interrupting Marv. "If we can get the players conscious of other positions, they may play better knowing we don't have enough personnel. Its a small thing, but I want them all conscious of the problem we have with depth of players. They all have to plan on playing the entire sixty minutes, we don't have enough personnel to do otherwise."

"Let's hope the game weather is cool. Hot weather would completely kill us." Marv said.

Linemen were shifted to various positions and evaluated. Slowly the group of players became a team. Other changes were decided upon as the talent of the team was constantly reviewed and re-evaluated by the coaches.

Essentially the beginning 1956 Augie team was the same personnel as had played the previous year. The main change was in positions of many of the men. But would it be better and would Augie win with these position changes? The members of the team thought so. The esprit-de-corps that was lacking in 1955 developed with a vengeance in 1956. A new attitude had been instilled in the players and the students by the time the first game rolled around in September 1956.

NCC MORE BALANCED THIS SEASON
Craig Stolze, ARGUS-LEADER sports editor,
sums up prospects in the North Central Conference for the 1956 season.

Sizing up the North Central Conference football scrap anytime is perilous. This year it appears even more hazardous.

Usually a well-balanced league in which any member is apt, on a given day, to take any other club, the NCC in 1956 appears better balanced than ever.

If South Dakota University can withstand the rigors of a tough schedule which doesn't find them at home until Dakota Day, we think "Boot" Stewart could "boot" home a winner in the first year. The Coyote backs can't be touched in the NCC.

South Dakota State, perennial powerhouse, can't be underestimated despite heavy losses from last year's champs. We pick them for second.

"Buck" Starbuck, at Iowa Teachers, is unusually optimistic and reports from Cedar Falls are that the Panthers are the team to beat. Halfbacks Pat Halligan and Clayton Thomas are outstanding. So is Dick Formanek, all - conference guard. We see the Tutors third.

North Dakota University, despite a mighty thin roster, gets our vote for fourth. Spearheaded by the conference's outstanding lineman—Little All-American Steve Myhra—the Sioux will be a rugged opponent for anybody. Dick McBride, leading scorer in the NCC last year, is back again.

Morningside may have the best line in the league. Dewy Halford has some good backs, too, but we have to put the Maroons behind the first four.

The one conference game Augustana won last year was over North Dakota State and we think the Oikles will finish ahead of the Bison again. A revivified Viking team should start its long climb uphill in the conference. There's plenty of size in the line, but the Oikles may lack the breakaway backfield speed necessary.

North Dakota State, undermanned with only 19 men answering the initial call, may benefit by the astute coaching of Les Luymes, but the Herd doesn't look like more than a cellar dweller to us.

Augustana was picked for the bottom again. So what's new?

The stage was set for the first game against Wayne State Teacher of Nebraska. The previous year they had fought to a draw, a 0—0 tie. Augie had nine first downs to Wayne States three, but they could not score a touchdown. No winners.

TONIGHT'S GAME:

*Phil Nelson will probably do a lot of work at the key quarterback spot. The big Minneapolis back has been showing good form on passing and running. Paul Heine and Bob Walton are good choices in the important end positions. Heine, a transferee from Hibbing Junior College, saw quite a bit of action in the end spot during last season, and Walton was given All-American rating when he played at Washington High School under Burns. *Augie football brochure*

The season began on Saturday night, September 15, 1956. The Augie Vikings took command from the beginning. Blocking and tackling with the fury of the Gods, Wayne State Teachers fell to the overwhelming power of the Norse gods. The contest was a resounding success for Augie. However the score of 27 to 6 wasn't conclusive enough to predict a winning season but the team had gotten off on the right foot by proving they could execute plays flawlessly and control the ball when they needed to.

The campus became alive with the thrill of the success and even the conservative element on the campus admitted that it was a good feeling to have finally won a athletic contest, even though they deplored the barbaric game of football. A half hour after the final gun of the game, the bell atop of Old Main began ringing. It continued for a hour before the campus police made them stop.

Quarterback Club—September 17, 1956

The following Monday noon Quarterback club was packed. Augie had won!

Burns: "I declare the 1956 Football season ended." Laughter. "We've beaten last years win record already." Laughter. "Everybody played well, and we were lucky to out score Wayne State. We didn't come out of the contest unharmed. Injuries, that's what will hurt us. Bill Simpson hurt his knee, Tom Rohwer is out for a while, but Terry Hokenstad is coming back to play after suffering his injury a couple of weeks ago. We played well but this week is going to be the real contest. North Dakota State is going to be tough. We beat them last year but I've heard from our scouts that they are out for blood this year. Don't let the sports casters prediction that ND State will be the 'cellar dweller' this year fool you. Never forget that they could be a spoiler in the league. We'll give them a good game, and I hope we'll win.

The Augie fans reacted to the win over Wayne State with a curious excitement. Was it true? We won? Didn't the other team show up? Slowly the win was accepted and pep-rallies were held to cheer the team on for the contest in North Dakota.

The high expectations of the campus, team players, and coaches proved to be short lived. The next game, this time against North Dakota State, proved to be a disaster for Augie's football team. Augie played hard but the North Dakota team had one of those days when nothing went wrong for them. Although North Dakota State had struggled for years and especially the week before, on this night they played and looked like they were in mid-season form of a winning team. They ran with abandon recklessness and at will against the Augustana line and they could not be stopped. Augie didn't just lose the game, they were humiliated by a score of 42 to 7. Apparently Coach Burns reputation hadn't reached North Dakota.

The bell atop Old Main remained quiet that Saturday.

Quarterback Club—September 24, 1956

Burns at the Quarterback Club on Monday at the Cottage:

"Now I know what it feels like to be hit by a bulldozer." Laughter. "Did anyone get the license number of that truck so I can report them?" Laughter. "ND State was good. Not only good, but superb. They came out of the chute running and never stopped. We were outmatched. We were out coached. I admit that. Their players outplayed us from the beginning, and we didn't know how to stop them. It was a long, quiet ride on the bus back to Augie. This week. What can I say?" Pause. "It's **band day**." Laughter. "The University is going to be tough. Last year they beat us, 35 to 18. Hell, they've beat Augie almost every game since I played for them. For the last ten years." Laughter. Then Burns looked at a sheet of paper. "In 1954 it was 33 to 6, in 1953 it was 33 to 0, in 1952 they walloped us 62 to 18, and in 1951 they outdid us by 54 to 7. They don't expect to let up on us this year." Nervous laughter. "The University has been predicted to win the conference, and they intend to achieve it over our bodies. I've heard that their coach didn't take very kindly to their loss to Nebraska last week. It has made him very mad and my scouts tell me that they're going to practice late every night this week. Their diet is going to consist of raw, red meat at every meal. We've got to stop their all-conference back, Duane Leach and Carl Johnson. They're the key to their offense. Leach scored two touchdowns last year against us, TWO. A 40 yard-pass from McDowell, and a 15-yard run. But listen to this, Ailts ran a 59-yarder and a 67 yarder. The U. ran a total of 249 yards against us, and passed for 111 yards. We've got to stop those types of runs. Augie had to score on short runs, Nelson 2 yards, Falgren 6 yards, and Howlin longest was 12 yards. Augie had to fight like mad just to score. And their 205 pound linemen can't be forgotten." Laughter. " Our line averages one hundred nine-ty pounds, and that's with their pads on." Roars of laughter. "With the exception of Phil Nelson weighing one hundred ninety pounds, our backfield averages one hundred sixty-five pounds. Hell, I weighted more than that when I was a baby." Laughter. "Remember it's band day this Saturday."

The practice session were intensive all week long. Humiliation can do that to you. Makes you humble. Licking their wounds all week, Phil Nelson and his charges prepared for the next weeks' game with South Dakota University.

Humiliating as their defeat at North Dakota had been, the student body and the community did not entirely lose faith in the Vikings. Everyone vowed that they would demonstrate their faith with an enthusiastic turnout at the next contest against the University. The defeat a year ago was not to be forgotten by the Norsemen.

Another added incentive to me was the fact that three of my former team-mates from WHS would be playing against me. Duane Leach, Jack Neuroth, and Jim Kolb were expected to play for the University on Saturday. The game became a matter of pride now. I had to win.

University of South Dakota

The night of the game proved to be a superb evening. A classic Fall evening had developed with mild weather, clear sky, and no wind. Ticket sales had been brisk and the beautiful evening increased the turn out of the local fans. Extra bleachers had been installed on the south side of the Augie field in anticipation of a good turnout. They filled up before the game began and many fans began standing along the sidelines. It turned out to be a sold-out game. More people were at Viking Stadium than had seen the previous twenty games combined. Sold out. At an Augie football game? Even the front office didn't know how many thousands of tickets had been sold. By the time of kick-off, the stands were overflowing and there was standing room only. Everyone sensed that history may be made tonight.

The University football players appeared confident. Confident to a point of being cocky, and a little obnoxious. Augie players who wandered onto their side of the field were jeered at by University fans. However the Augie players were not cowed under by these jibes. I kept remembering that Augie had not beaten the University since 1942. 1942!

The Augie players warmed up slowly. They watched with interest the U players warming up. As the warm-ups progressed, the University supporters began to sense the change of mood at Augustana and they began to tone down their jibes. Maybe Augie can beat us tonight many confided to each other.

The Augie players were more confident than the University fans in the stands had figured them for at first. A higher pitch of dedication began developing in the minds of the cheerleaders. They began yelling louder and louder, and the confidence in them flowed into the stands. The fans caught the fever of confidence. They wanted the contest to begin.

It was a exciting game from the start. Augustana didn't concede anything to the University. Their touchdowns were matched by our touchdowns. Augie was playing over their head. Augie matched block for block, tackle for tackle and when it was over, Augie had won. Augustana had upset the University. We had won by a score of 14 to 12. It was a fabulous upset win for us. The game was so close that the fans and the team were not completely sure of success until the final gun sounded. Phil Nelson's coolly kicked two extra points after two touchdowns and these became the margin of success. Augustana had beaten the University! Augie had beaten the potential conference champs. Augie knocked the 'U' from their pedestal.

The bell at Old Main began ringing almost before the gun sounded at the end of the game. Having had little opportunity in a number of years to ring the Old Main bell that announced victories of the football team, the bell ringing didn't stop for hours. Finally the neighborhood residents called the police to have it stopped.

Quarterback Club—Monday, October 1, 1956

Coach Burns: "Read the Argus-Leader headlines Saturday: Vikings Stun Coyotes 14-12. Stunned the Coyotes? Hell, Augie stunned the hell out of me. And I'm the coach. Is this my team?" (laughter). "As you saw it was a close one...but we came out ahead. I'll take them any way I can get them. This was the first win over the University of South Dakota since 1942. Its been a long drought. The only thing that dampened my spirit was when the campus police arrested me for ringing the Old Main bell too long." (Laughter). "Really, I'd like to give each of the ones who were ringing the bell on Saturday night a big kiss. They did a wonderful job. And the team. What more can you ask of a team? Our line was superb. They out-gunned the U all night. Seven minutes into the game, our line held them on their twelve-yard line. Held them! Then our defense became the offense and ran the ball down their throat. Howlin's 38-yard run really caught them off-guard. Howlin has to run, he's too damn small to stand being caught by those big linemen. One tackle and he says he wouldn't be able to get up. Nelson's extra point was perfect. That toe was the difference. First Quarter: Seven to zip. The U. didn't think we were real. Howlin's fantastic catch in the second quarter kept the..., what was it? a 75-yard march—from our 20 yard line—put the ball on the 5-yard line and Arlo Feiock's plunge over from the one really iced it. Nelson's toe for the extra point was near perfection. Fourteen to zip

116

now and the gun sounded. Two points! My heart almost couldn't stand it. And the last point went through the goal posts by only a foot. I could almost kiss Phil. No, they only do that in San Francisco." Laughter. "Next week I'm going to make sure his shoes are polished before the game. By me. (laughter) If that's what it takes."

"The second-half really demonstrated the character of the line. Defense all the way. We couldn't get the offense going well enough to punch in another score. When Harry Nauffs from the U. recovered the fumble on the 43, right after the half, I really didn't know what to expect. I knew we had a defense, but going both ways can wear you out. And it did. Luckily they missed their extra point, both times. 14 to 12 can give a coach heartburn. The line really gave their best.

"Next week, we play State. At Brookings. We've never beaten the Jackrabbits, here or up there. Never. And they're on their own turf. Hope to see you up there."

....

All of the following week, there was nothing but talk of the game with the University. The campus was alive with football fever. A prayer was said by President Stavig at Chapel and a spontaneous rally broke out in the gym. To have beaten the 'U' was success beyond belief—a goal never to be emitted aloud by the student body but never-the-less harbored in their secret prayers. Everyone on campus walked a lot more erect and heads were held higher during that week. After years of dismal defeats, at long last it was proven that Augie could compete in this Conference. But could this be repeated ever again, or was this a fluke?

Caught in the action of a stimulating yell are the cheerleaders for the 1956-57 athletic season.
Dave Johnson, Mitchell; Dick Erickson, Sioux Falls; Wayne Mitchell, Sioux Falls; Dean Larsen, Hazard, Nebr.; and Ordelle Hill, Canton.
Kneeling are Marilyn LeClaire, St. Paul; Verna Skarsten, Benson, Minn., Pat Jorgensen, Sioux Falls; Joan Sorensen, Sioux Falls; and Soffie Hoines, Langford.

Overwhelming support from the public, fans, and cheerleaders spurred the 1956 Augie football players on.

The sheer determination and will power of the backfield (Jon Falgren, Roger Rygh, Phil Nelson, and Chuck Howlin) kept Augie in the winning column.

Lawrence Serena Willy Jane Heither Janet Lee Lane • Roy Marie Horn Shirley Margie Lane • Hugh Rose Ann O'Neil James Cathryn John Hugh Carrie ViLettie Lintner Ruby Elmer Fredricks Darold 'Dick' Fredricks Lane • Carol Larson • Dean Larson • Marilyn LeClaire • Carolee Leffert • Lee Avis Kruse Delores Parker Joan Pedersen June Ranney Lehman • Muriel Leivestad • Luther Lerseth • Ray Leu • Duane Lewis • Darrel Lidel • Connie Lien • Norbert Limmer • Sheila Linahan • Mary Lindekugel • Frances Line • Charles Lockhart • Mary Lofswold • Arlene Hoefert Lofswold • Marie Loken • Dick Lokken • Janet Olson Lokken • Margaret Loomis • Bill Lowe • Laura Lucas • Patricia Luhrs • Darrel Lundby • Florence Lyng • Edith Mabee • Gladys Machmiller • Maureen Mahlen • Joe Mancuso • Dean Mann • Bill Mannion • Constance Marsh • John Marshman • Patricia Masters • Barbara Mathers • Bill Mathers • Leona Matthies • Melvin Matthies • Barb Mattison • DeWayne Matz • Joanne Maurstad • Marilyn Mavity • Patricia McCabe • Howard McCabe • Bobby McClare • Ron McConnell • Tom McGowan • Joan McGuire • Lloyd McKenzie • Tom McKeon • John McLaughlin • June Parrish McNally • John Ted Medin • Joy Bishop Mehlhaff • Richard 'Dick' Lois Paulson Merrill • Marlene Michael • Constance Miller • Dale Miller • Maxine Brewer Miller • Janet Picasso Missner • Harold Mitchell • Wanda Mitchell • Wayne Mitchell • Robert Moe • George Alice Art Myrtle Helen Mildred Lester Esther Mofle • Robert Esther Lyle Harold Girt Shirley Mofle • Marilyn Molskness • Robert Monahan • Chuck Hill Audrey Larry Edna Colwell Monger • Kent Morstad • Marjorie Mulvey • Earl Pamela Susan Paul Mundt • Dona Murray • Sandra Murray • Robert Myklebust • Marce Myhra • Daniel Nachel • Carl Naessig • Gene Sam Tim Nash • Phillip Natwick • Paul Natwick • Robert Naylor • Dick Ron Neish • Phillip Nelson • Janet Nelson • John Nelson • Lucile Nelson • Wesley Nelson • Dr. Ron Nelson • Walter Nelson • Robert Nervig • Janice Neshiem • Jean Nessan • Joan Neuheisel • Ben Newcomb • Bob Newcomb • Patricia Nielsen • Kenneth Noel • Cindy Nold • John Norberg • Carole Nordseth • Bill Norton • Mildred Becker Nuffer • James Ode • Elmer Odland • Dorrine Ogdie • Patricia Ogle • Dave Oien • Raymond Oistad • Curt Olsen • Gerald Olsen • Gordon Olson • Janet Olson • Ruth Thoms Olson • Merilyn Olsen

continued on page 120

119

James Ontjes • Dolores Orpen • Allan Osmann • Verlyn Oveson • James Page • Hyung Woong Pak • Dona Palmer • Elmer Parish • Juanita Park • Joelene Parks • Gwili Kay Pasco • Shirley Paul • Dorothy Paulsen • Lois Paulson • Larry Pawlowski • Warren Pay • Nancy Pennock • Bud Perkins • Joan Perrenoud • Lester Pereboom • Don Petersen • Richard Peterson • Roger Peterson • Patricia Peterson • Maxine Hansen Peterson • Jacqueline Petty • Clinton Philips • Mary Poland • Bill Polzien • Zane Prang • Floyd Prouty • Vivian Prouty • Della Pulflord • David Quanbeck • Minerva Quinell • Helen Rallis • Chris Rallis • BarBara Ramsey • Bill Hugh Ranney • Jim Ratzloff • Mrs Earl Rea • Marcine Reiners • Ray Reiners • Don Renner • Janet Rensberger • John Reppe • Elaine Turley Riemann • Donna Ring • Don Harold Ritter • Max Rittgers • Ed Roberts • Jim Robertson • Avis Rodness • Richard Roe • Steve Paul Rogness • Leona Ohlman Rohrer • Glenn Rollag • Dick Ronken • Virginia Rood • Gloria Bradley Rose • Richard Thomas Rose • Carol Rote • Fern Rubin • Dolores Runeberg • Dorothy Wilson Rupp • Patricia Rustad • Donna Rutili • Curtis Ruud • Michael Ryan • Roger Rygh • Lillian Berreth Betty Coulter Verna Miller George Hank Charles Sachen • Ann Sachen Stratmeyer • Donald Salberg • Pamela Schuldt Sampson • Doretta Sanders • Roy Satre • James Schamber • Joan Scheinost • Donald Schmeyer • Carole Schlunsen • Katie Kinney Schmidt • Beverly Schmidt • Donna Schmidt • Agnes Schroeder • Jerry Schryver • Bob Schuck • Richard Schuldt • Bob Dick Duane Delores Kenny Les Schuldt • Clayton Jerry Scott • Garry Scott • Dorothy Selken • Hazel Seloover • Arlan Selland • Doyle Selland • Glenn Sellevold • Lavonne Seubert • Velda Severson • Lois Severtson Morris • Jack 'Chub' Shafer • Eddie Harold Shafer • Wanda Shelp • Marlene Shelton • Anne Shepler • Robert Sheppard • Marlene Shields • Mary Siekmeier • Paul Siewert • Florence Sikkink • Malvis Simkins • Bill Chuck Robert Cora Simpson • John Simko • Marion Sisson • Dale Don Vern Skadsen • Marilyn Skaggs • Arlen Skinner • Marian Slob • Don Small • Eleanor Small • Carolyn Smith • Delmar Smith • June Smith • Pat Smith • Don Smithback • Richard Smith • S. E. Smithlin • Robert Solem • Robert Souter • Maxine Clark Snook • Darrell Kenneth Snook • Dean Songstad • Celia Evelyn Kraft Jean Miller Helen Schultz Ernestine DePew Roger Sordrager

continued on page 138

9
More surprises for the fans

In 1951, South Dakota State had beaten Augustana by a score of 58 to 7. In 1955 the score had been 28 to 0. I couldn't forget these games. I wouldn't. The games had been humiliating to me as a freshman and again as a junior but this year, as a senior, I felt extremely confident that Augie was going to win. Augie had never beaten State at football and I vowed that this was to be the year it would happen.

The contest was to be held in Brookings. State had been pegged for second place in the league and the word was out that they were not going to lose to Augie. South Dakota State had been humiliated by a big loss, 60 to 0, to Arizona the week before. They were out for revenge. Augie was going to get all of the punishment this team could give. They had continually dominated Augie games in the past with large point margins and State was determined to do it again.

During the week before the contest, the Augie players practiced with a diligence and determination never seen here before. The players felt that they could give State a good showing even though they were out-manned two to one in personnel. Problems were beginning to show, however, from having too few players. Injuries were beginning to hamper Augie. I had a pulled groin muscle in the University game and Coach Burns was concerned that I wouldn't play in the State game. I was in so much pain on Monday, I couldn't practice. Tuesday and Wednesday I was better but the coach kept me on the field dressed in sweat clothes to watch the team drill. By Thursday I was feeling better so Coach Burns had me go through the drills with the team at half-pace, hoping that no one would get injured. He couldn't afford to lose any more players.

If you can meet with triumph and disaster and treat those two impostors just the same.

Saturday came and the team gathered at Augie to board the bus for the trip to Brookings. It seemed like a long 60 mile ride but we kept focused only on the game. This was for real. This was it. The past had to be atoned for.

We did our pregame warm-ups in a stadium that was filled to capacity. There was standing room only. The Governor—Joe Foss—was there. Six-thousand eight hundred fans in the stands were screaming for blood—Augie blood. The sound of yells and cheers by fans were deafening.

From the start of the game, me and the other Augie players played with a passion never before seen by the fans. Slant right, slant left, pass over the center to Walton...we kept hammering away. The State players were stunned. We had the ball and we moved it down the field. We scored on a pass from

Nelson to Jones. Jones had a bloody face and a broken nose but he still caught the ball for the touchdown. Phil kicked the extra point. Seven to nothing—Augie was ahead. State then took the ball and came at us with everything they had. It was a barnburner of a contest. We continued to outsmart, outplay, and outscore State, however and when the contest ended, **Augie had beaten State by a score of 21 to 20.** Again the margin of victory was Phil Nelson's toe. Augustana had beat State as well as the University for the first time, and in the same season. The total point difference was three, but it was enough.

On the return night bus trip of Sioux Falls, on Highway 77, the players settled down to rest and quietly absorb the fruits of their success. After leaving Brookings I sat back in my seat and relaxed. It had been a hard fought game and I was tired.

As the city limits of Sioux Falls was approached the coaches decided to change the routine. Normally the bus and players would return to the Augie campus after a game, but this time the bus driver was instructed by Coach Burns to drive up and down Phillips Avenue and Main before returning to the Augie campus. What a spectacle the caravan presented as it made its way through the city with horns blaring and lights blinking. After two runs up and down the streets, the bus returned to the Augie campus.

The Old Main bell was ringing. An impromptu rally was held after the bus unloaded at the gymnasium. Coach Burns waxed eloquently as he praised the student body and the team.

The next day, all of the Augie campus and the City of Sioux Falls were bubbling with the news of the events that had happened in Brookings. Although many students at Augie were engrossed only in academic pursuit at the college, this event was an impact on their lives. *Augie had created the upset of the decade and they had to admit that it felt good to be thought of as something more that cannon fodder for the Midwest.* Augie was developing pride. Pride was felt in even the here-to-for uninvolved Augie student.

On Monday the mad rush for game tickets began. The telephones rang off their hooks at the athletic department. Peggy Jones, Bob Burn's student secretary went into full time status as she tried to cope with the demands of the public for tickets to the next game with Iowa State Teachers College. Organization of ticket numbering had to be done by hand as there was no machine to do the work and she pressed her father and others into hand stamping the numbers on thousands of tickets. It was a heady situation that involved the entire athletic department. Peggy quickly found out that she had acquired many new 'friends'. 'Friends' that wanted tickets to the game.

Quarterback Club October 8, 1956

Monday Quarterback Club at the Cottage; Burns: "What a shoot-out. Two plays before Jones scored our first touchdown, he laid a block on a big player across from him. A crab-block, you know, arm around the legs. Well, Jones happened to be slow in letting the player up so the State player punched him in the face. Full force. Square in the face. Jones was stunned. Blood was squirting all over the place. His face was a mess when he came over to the bench and asked if he could be taken out to get his face repaired. Hell, I didn't have any replacement for him, so I told him to 'Shake it off." He ran back into the huddle still dripping blood. The referee on the sideline, standing next to me, looked at me and said I had a hell of a way with my players, and he left shaking his head in disbelief. Next play Nelson called a pass to Jones. Jones looked at Nelson and said he didn't feel he could catch anything, he felt his nose was broken, and the blood was still flowing out of his nose. Nelson looked at Jones, straight in the eyes, and said to Jones—'Shake it off.' The pass was perfect. Jones scored from 25-yards out on the pass. Now that's a football player...and I have ten others like him. Great men. Great team.

"That touchdown was set up by the drive we did after Dick Raddaiz punted into the end zone. We took it on the twenty and drove to the 25 where we were stopped. I felt we should try something different so I had them try that field goal from the 31. No good. Nelson failed but he redeemed himself by intercepting a pass by the Jacks two plays later. That set up Jones score on that fabulous pass with a little over four minutes left in the Quarter. Seven to zip. That score looked great on the scoreboard. Now we had to contain them, stop them from scoring too many touchdowns. I took Jones out long enough to clean his face off. (faint laughter).

Second Quarter was a long quarter for me. After Lee Kragenbring scored for State, I thought 'Here it comes now. They can't be stopped now.' I couldn't believe it. Nelson and Fredricks both got into the backfield on the point after and blocked the extra point. I've looked at the film we took at the game a dozen times and I still can't see how they both got across the line and into the backfield. But they did. 7 to 6. After we took the ball, Kragenbring must have been really mad because he intercepted a pass. His interception and run back by the Jacks really hurt us. And then that penalty by us put the ball on their one. I've looked over the film a dozen times and I still can't see the personal foul. You win some, and you lose some. But this one hurt because it allowed them to get a score. At that point it was 13 to 7 with a little over three minutes in the half.

We did call a time out after Nelson passed to Heine and we were on the twelve yard line. (Burns showed a lot of irritation in his voice now). I can see it in the film. It shows up clear that we signaled for a time out. That referee just wanted to take a pee at half-time and he was in a hurry to get off of the field. That's why I had to argue with him. Luckily the other referee agreed with me. I knew we probably couldn't score, but it was worth the try. Howlin made it to the three before he was pulled down. Sure made the State coach mad when they had to come back from the locker room to do that one play. They were cold by then but it didn't help us. I couldn't let the referee or State get away without paying for their mistake.

It was 13 to 7 at the half. Man I was really wondering how we could survive the second half. A number of my players were hurting with injuries—especially Jones whose nose had swollen up. We just had to tape it and we got a helmet with a face-guard for him but he wouldn't wear it. Said it blocked his view.

Arlo Feiock's score put us back in the game after five minutes into the third Quarter, and Nelson booted the extra point—14 to 13, our lead. I've got to mention one thing that really helped us. Phil's quick-kicks on three occasions kept the pressure on State. Those perfect quick-kicks kept State off balance. With Nelson's height, physical ability to punt, and the strong line ahead of him to hold out the State players, we had the ability to keep State off balance a lot of the time.

Until about eleven minutes were left, we held onto our own. Then Feiock's four-yard plunge on that counter-play did the trick. You know, we could never get that counter-play to work in practice against our 'black shirts' that Neuser Salem coaches, but it worked in the game. Next week I'm going to look at all of the plays we fail to complete in practice and start the game with them against Iowa State Teachers. (laughter).

The score was 21 to 13, our favor. Bob Newcomb played a great game. His recovery of State's fumble on their 44 gave us some breathing time. Nelson put them in the hole on his quick-kick again after we were stopped by their defense. That gave me about ten seconds of recovery time before my next heart murmur was felt. State scared the hell out of me when they scored on their 77 yard drive. That Nig Johnson reception (Burns lowers his head and shakes it)—I had a nightmare about that last night. 21 to 20 and over three minutes left. But we were able to run out the clock. This was the first win ever by Augie over the Jackrabbits.

"This week. It's Homecoming Week! We should have had it last week to celebrate our 21 to 20 win over the State game. One point! One point. I'm going to buy Phil Nelson a complete new set of shoes for the Homecoming game against Iowa State Teachers. We'll need it. In the past five homecoming games, our opponents have outscored Augie 176 points to Augie's 7, and those seven were scored five years ago, when Fredricks and Walton first played here. They left, went into the services, and now they're back. Lets hope they are the difference this week. Last year Iowa Teachers outscored Augie 28 to 7. Need I say more?"

Augie Homecoming—1956

Augustana's Vikings Seek to End Homecoming Drought:

The football picture at Augustana has taken on a brighter hue than it has had in quite awhile. There is much optimism as "Ole the Viking" is readying his charges to bring victory to Augie in their annual gridiron battle.

Although the actual team personnel has not been changed to a great extent over against last year's squad, the use of the personnel has. With a few additions from junior colleges and a shifting of returning players, Coach Bob Burns hopes to find a unit capable of operating his multiple offense.

As the festivities of Homecoming are centered around the game, nothing but a victory will make Viking Days complete. The Oles will be shooting for their first victory in their last eight homecoming games. It is a case of the seven lean years and now, proverbially, the seven fat years should appear.

The Viking line is not overly large, but should be able to hold its own very well. At the ends Bob Walton and Paul Heine (who was Augie's leading pass catcher last year) hold down the top spots. Behind them are Vern Broughton, Don Jones, and Jim Ratzloff.

As the season progresses many changes may be made, especially in the tackles and guards. The tackles have been Ken Richards and Carl Guthals. Guthals could well become the Oikles' best lineman. Ready for action at any time if these boys slack up are Terry Hokenstad and John Berven.

Dick Fredricks and Bill Simpson, both from Sioux Falls, fill out the guard slots with Jim Westby, Tom Rohwer, and Steve Rogness pushing them for a starting position.

At the middle of the line Bob Newcomb is top man and also a linebacker. Ready with assistance are Paul Rogness and Dick Boettcher, both lettermen.

The backfield is manned by small breakaway runners, such as Chuck Howlin, Roger Rygh, Arlo Feiock, Lloyd McKenzie, and Jon Falgren. They are all centered around quarterback Phil Nelson who is very versatile, having played three positions. Gayle Dietz is ready at a moment's notice to step in and run the team.

*With this bunch of football players, Coach Burns hopes to lead Augie on her long climb up the North Central Conference ladder to more respectable position. Adding more each year, the Oikles may someday occupy the top rung, but before this comes Augie's first homecoming victory in eight years. SKOL! *Augie football brochure*

Barbara Cummings was elected Homecoming Queen. She was to preside over her court of beauties: Sharon Frank, Diane Johnson, Connie Lien, Lois Paulson, Donna Ring, and June Smith. Amid the darkness of night at the

Her Majesty . . .
Barbara Cummings

Sharon Frank

Diane Johnson

Connie Lien

Lois Paulson

Donna Ring

June Smith

126

football stadium, Barbara and her court were presented to the campus. Everyone felt good. They knew the Queen and court might reign over a historical happening never experienced at Augie. Expectation for a winning game was high.

VIKING DAYS 1956: Welcome to Viking Days, 1956...since 1924, this football game has been the focal point in the homecoming tradition of Augustana. Color and gaiety spark the campus today as activities get into full swing...Chairman Paul Rogness has coordinated the homecoming activities, bringing together an interesting mixture of the new and the traditional, in hopes of making Viking Days a memorable occasion in your mind.

Lending color to the campus today is a new innovation of Viking Days, landed floats. The six brother-sister societies constructed these floats at various prominent places on the campus under a competitive basis. Judging took place last night, and the winners will be announced during the half-time ceremonies.

Flying over the stadium for the very first time are the colors of the seven schools of the North Central Conference. These flags, a permanent decoration for Viking Stadium, have been donated by the Viking Days committee.

During the pre-game ceremonies you will be meeting our lovely Queen. She and her court will be presented to the audience.

Immediately following the tussle between the Vikings and Panthers of Iowa State Teachers, another battle will commence a few hundred yards away, a battle equally grim and tense: the soph versus frosh Tug-of-War will determine the status of the freshmen once and for all. If the sophomores are dragged through the slough of mud, the beanies come off...if the freshmen are drenched, then the "wearing of the green" will continue for another week.

Beginning at four-thirty, the annual Smorgasbord will be held in the gymnasium. Tickets will be available at the door.

*Closing the festivities for Saturday will be the traditional Viking Varieties. When the curtain rises at 8:15 in the gym, the Rub-a-dubs will capture your laughs as they take you through the two-hour performance of the best talent on the college campus. Coordinating the varied acts will be the Augie-renowned Northlanders, who are planning a semi-back-ground music routine for the show. *Augie football brochure*

It was a extraordinary week on campus and it became wild as the Saturday game approached. Rallies were held and routine weekend trips home were canceled as nothing could be missed on campus. The very thought of underdog Augie winning another game was worth the price of not going home for a weekend. Anyway somebody was needed to stay on campus to ring that victory bell in Old Main. It had become the scourge of the neighborhood and the citizens in the neighborhoods around Augie had enough of it. They wanted it stopped. (Fat chance).

Iowa State Teachers College

Today's Game: Today's game will mark the entrance of Iowa State Teachers, one of the pre-season favorites, into the NCC race in which Augustana has already played three games, the last two being victories over highly-rated SDU and SD State.

The Panthers, who have a 9 win—1 loss record for last year, are undefeated so far this season. They have a well-balanced attack and are dangerous in both running and passing. Their line will out-weigh the Vikings approximately fifteen pounds per man.

The Vikings, fresh from winning a 21-20 thriller from SD State College last Saturday, will have the advantage of their home field as well as that all-winning homecoming spirit. Augie's starting line-up will be much the same as it was against SD State.

The Panthers line will be led by Dick Formanek, 180 lb. senior, who was all-conference last year. Sports writers rate him as one of the top linemen in the conference. Their backfield will be sparked by halfbacks, Thomas and Holligan and fullback Brinkley.

*Carrying the brunt of the load for Augustana will be its stalwart, iron-man line, which against State and the U turned in sixty-minute performances. They include Walton, Jones, Guthals, Hokenstad, Richards, Fredricks, and Bob Newcomb. *Augie football brochure*

Again a miracle happened. A hard-fought game with Iowa State Teacher ended in a victory for Augie. Augie had won again, this time by the score of 13 to 6. This put Augie in contention for the championship for the first time since the early 1940s when Lefty Olson coached the squad.

10
The Championship Game–Morningside

Augie had beaten Wayne State Teachers, South Dakota University, South Dakota State, Iowa State Teachers, and Graceland. A record had been set for Augie—three conference games had been won. The following week, however, was to be a game against Morningside of Sioux City that would determine the championship.

Morningside was a powerhouse. They were unbeaten although the game with Iowa Teachers had ended in a tie. This tie could make the difference in the championship title if Augustana beat them. Morningside was good enough to take the championship away from the Cinderella team from Sioux Falls but they could not take the excitement and enthusiasm that had surrounded Augie since the beginning of the year. The underdog Augustana College's football team had won the hearts of the fans in the Midwest.

"Coach, let me read this article from the Argus." Kessinger said as Burns walked into the office. "It's by the Associated Press: *The clock may strike twelve for the Cinderella team of Augustana College this weekend, but don't bet any money on it.*

The Vikings will be out to do what anyone would have described this summer as preposterous—take over the lead of the North Central Conference.

They go against Morningside's Maroons in Sioux City and a victory would give them a small margin because the Maroons had a perfect record sullied by a tie with Iowa Teachers Saturday.

Whether they could go on and win the championship even if they win the big one against Morningside remains to be seen, however, since they must meet North Dakota University the week after the Maroon game."

"I'm not going to show up this Saturday." Burns quipped. "Let them find us. If we forfeit the game, we will still be in second place. Then we can face North Dakota U in a rested condition and fight to retain our second place."

"We can't do that," Kessinger shot back.

"Their defense has allowed only two touchdowns in their last five wins." Rist said.

"I've got it all figured out." Burns suddenly blurted out. "Let's leak it to the press that Morningside broke into the office last night and stole all of our plays for the game against them. That way if we lose, everybody will forgive us."

"Broke into our office? We were here all last night. Nobody would believe us." Kessinger protested.

"That's just the point, it's so absurd it will be believed. We have too many key injuries to play the championship game this week. We're going to be massacred."

....

ON THE CAMPUS: Dr. L. M. Stavig recently announced that the New Men's Dormitory will be formally known as SOLBERG HALL. The decision was made by the board of directors during a meeting held early in October.

SOLBERG HALL is named in honor of Charles Orrin Solberg, president of Augustana College and Normal School from 1920-28.

....

"You going to the championship game this weekend?"

"Are you kidding. I wouldn't miss it for the world. Morningside's undefeated and has its eyes on the championship. Their first outright championship in 33 years."

"That Burns. What a coach. I heard he may go to Notre Dame next. He won't stay at Augie long if he pulls a win out of this game this weekend."

"Should be the best game of the year. Better get your tickets right away, I hear there aren't many left. The place is going to be sold out."

Morningside College—Championship game

	North Central Conference standings			
	win	loss	tie	%
Morningside	3	0	1	.875
Augustana	3	1	0	.750
SD University	2	2	0	.500
SD State	1	2	0	.333
ND State	1	2	0	.333
ND University	1	3	0	.250
Iowa Teachers	0	1	1	.250

....

The players knew what the Morningside contest meant. This was it , the last chance for Augie to win the championship. Morningside's first outright championship was in 1923, 33 years ago, the year the league was organized. The championship had eluded them ever since then. They wanted it bad. Augustana had never won it. Or even gotten this close to winning it. In fact they had never been close in the running for it.

There was little talking or fooling around by any of the players on the bus trip to Sioux City that Saturday. Ninety miles of silence. Players were reviewing their assignments. Chuck and Phil reviewed each other about different plays they would use in given situations. They had to be right. The bus stopped at the football stadium and the players got out, stretched themselves, and walked to the gate. The gate was unlocked and Coach Burns and Rist walked onto the field, followed by the players. Silence greeted them. The stadium was empty. The coaches and team walked around the field, side-line to side-line to get the feel of where the battle was to be fought. Satisfied, they returned to the bus and got on. The locker rooms where they were to change for the game was a short distance away.

The scene was set. There was no turning back, and there'd be no excuses. Winner take all, now or never. The Maroons were undefeated and they were confident that they could win. The championship was on the line.

The first quarter ended with neither team scoring and neither had attained momentum for a score. Hard defensive ball was being played by both teams. Then Morningside got hot and scored in the second quarter on a 30-yard run by Dutch Bryan. The score was 7 to 0 after the extra point was booted. Morningside was ahead when the second quarter ended.

During the half, Coach Burns and Coach Rist went around to the players and checked on their condition. Neither one said much. There was no criticism of the players. Both coaches knew that the players were giving their all and at this point in the season the main difference in winning would be the coaching. The Augie players tried to relax and rest-up for what they knew would be a grueling second half.

The half was over, and Morningside came out and took over the game. Bob Reynders snared a Nelson pass and Morningside scored. The extra point was good. Morningside was ahead by two touchdowns—14 to 0. It was a defensive game by both teams for the next fifteen minutes. Finally Augie's defense stopped Morningside on Augie's 22 yard line and Phil Nelson got hot on passing. Four passes to end Bob Walton put Augie on the one-yard line where Arlo Feiock carried it over for a score. Nelson's extra-point was good. With the score 14 to 7, the Augie players felt that they had a excellent chance at winning. I was confident that we could win. We had always gotten stronger as the game progressed. Due to our lack of depth, we knew we had to pace ourselves for the entire game but when the end was in sight, we gave it our all. This had worked in almost every game so far this season.

Gayle Dietz kicked off after our score. Morningside returned the punt to their 30 yard line. Then a totally unexpected occurred—Coach Burns pulled the entire first defensive team off of the field to give us a rest. A rest! We never took a rest. We didn't need a rest. We knew where we were going. I couldn't believe it as we walked off of the field and the second string players took over our positions. I knew it was a big opportunity for Morningside and the Morningside coach immediately recognized it. As the first string players watched from the sideline, Delaine Koch, Morningside's halfback, started a play that came toward the Augie bench. He had the ball. After turning the corner not over ten yards from Coach Burns, he broke away for a 70-yard run down the sideline. He scored a touchdown. Now Morningside had a 21 to 7 advantage.

We were devastated but Augie was not going to fold. On the second play after getting the ball, Phil Nelson passed to Jon Falgren and the play ended up on the 9-yard line—a 51 yard gain. But no. It was called back. Somebody on our team had been offside. A potential touchdown wiped out due to a off-side. However Augie then began a 76-yard drive toward the goal line. Howlin broke away for a 44-yard sprint at one time and we scored The extra point try by Nelson was blocked by Maroon Bob Puff. The score: 21 to 13. There was only 58 seconds left on the clock.

Time ran out before the Vikings could score again.

The hard fought game ended in Augie losing 21 to 13. Morningside had taken the championship away from the Cinderella team from Sioux Falls. Although we lost the championship, we had gained the respect and admiration of the fans of the Heartland.

....

North Dakota University
(The last Augie football game at Viking Stadium)

TODAY'S GAME: Today the Vikings will be attempting to finish higher in the conference than they have in the past 17 years.

North Dakota University, the foe for this game, a revamped ball club, found itself in the last stages of the season after losing three heartbreakers. In the opening game of the season they lost to Montana State, present champions of the Rocky Mountain Conference. They lost to South Dakota State College by one, and after leading Morningside, present conference champs, 3-0, the Sioux went down to defeat as a pass was intercepted and the Maroons took the game 7-3. In the last two tussles the NoDaks scored wins against North Dakota State and Iowa State Teachers, and will be gunning for 3-3 position in the conference.

NDU has the best lineman, in Steve Myhra, All-Conference and Little-All-American. A good passing game will be witnessed with Piasecki passing and McBride and Ryan receiving.

It will be interesting to see if the Vikings will be able to rebound from their conference championship battle with Morningside last week. While defeated 21-

13, the team gave a very good account of itself, breaking through the stiff Maroon line to score two touchdowns. Prior to the Augie-Maroon tussle, this line had allowed only one touchdown.

Today will mark the end of college football for eleven Vikings, Bill Simpson, Ken Richards, Paul Heine, Dick Fredricks, Phil Nelson, Don Jones, Ben and Bob Newcomb, Dick Boettcher, Roger Rygh and Chuck Howlin. When Burns blows the initial whistle for the spring drills, he will find a big gap in his present line with Richards, Fredricks, Jones, and Newcomb all making the final bow. All of these men, composing one of the best walls in recent Augustana football history, have been mainstays in the Burns' line-up.

Roger Rygh, fullback of the Viking Club, has proved an asset on the defensive team. Howlin, with his fancy running antics and strong desire in the defensive game, will leave a spot hard to fill in the Augie starting line-up. Nelson, one of the leading kickers in the conference, has proved his worth both offensively and defensively as he called the Oikles to a 5-2 season. Burns will also be on the look-out this spring for men to replace the reserve strength lost by the graduation of Simpson, Ben Newcomb, and Boettcher. *Augie football brochure

The following week Augie met North Dakota University. Little All American Steve Myhra was playing his last game for NDU. Although he played a good game, their team lost to Augie—26 to 14.

Craig Stolze, Argus-Leader Sports Editor summarizes the game in this Sunday November 4, 1956 article:

'Howitzer' Howlin Hits Sioux Club

Chuck Howlin made his home farewell a memorable one as he twisted and squirmed for 238 yards to lead the Augustana College Vikings to a 26-14 North Central football victory over the University of North Dakota here yesterday.

Howlin, a 160-pound mite who hails from Grand Forks, bailiwick of the Sioux, ran wild as the Oikles wound up their NCC season with a 4-2 record. The victory gave them a certain tie for runner-up honors behind Morningside.

In a battle of offenses the Sioux took a 14-13 advantage into the fourth quarter only to see the fired-up Vikings score two touchdowns in that period.

Howlin, a senior who barely got into the game at Grand Forks against this same club a year ago, was all over the field. He scored two of the Viking touchdowns, one on a 20-yard scamper.

The Sioux, with soph quarterback Steve Piasecki ever dangerous with his passing and running, junior left half Howard Grumbo rambling viciously and the great Steve Myhra performing magnificently on both defense and offense, turned in a fine game.

Statistics	Augie	NDU
First Downs	24	17
Yards rushing	371	308
Passes tried	5	14
Passes completed	3-35	5-71
Had intercepted	0	1
Fumbles lost	2	2

It was a combination of factors which shoved Augie to its sixth win of the season. Coupled with Howlin's running was a fine effort by the line and the appearance of regular quarterback Phil Nelson in the third period.

Nelson, who spent the night in a local hospital with illness, came off the bench to spark the two final Oikle tallies, scoring one of them himself.

Opportune substituting of a couple of fleet reserves, Lloyd McKenzie of Williston, N.D., and Roger Rygh of Roseau, Minn., helped, too. The tiny tandem of the 155 pound McKenzie and the 165 pound Rygh was the driving force in the touchdown drive which "untied" the score. They were sent in to "spell" the hard-working Howlin and fullback Arlo Feiock.

Not to be forgotten, too, is Gayle Dietz, 175-pound junior from Russell, Kans., who stepped into Nelson's vacant shoes at quarterback and did a fine job.

Augustana scored first. They punched over a touchdown with five minutes left in the opening stanza with Howlin going the final two yards. The Vikings had driven from their own 19 after NDU was held on fourth down.

Terry Hokenstad broke through to spill Piasecki there with fourth and one and the Vikings unfurled their first drive.

A 20-yard run by Howlin and a 27-yard pass from Jon Falgren to Howlin were the big gainers in the march.

Howlin finally went the last two yards to score and Nelson hustled in with his warm-up jacket on to kick the conversion.

North Dakota didn't waste much time tieing it. In four plays after the next kickoff they had a touchdown.

Grumbo reeled off 34 yards behind Myhra's blocking to the Augie 8, and after a penalty, Piasecki threw a 13-yard scoring aerial to towering end Bob Gilsdorf. Myhra kicked the extra point to tie it at 7-7.

Augustana bounced back into the lead early in the second period. Feiock went three yards to score after the Burnsmen drove 63 yards. Nelson's place-kick missed.

The Sioux soared into the lead shortly after when Grumbo ran 25 yards to score after tackle Garvin Stevens had recovered an Augie fumble on the Viking 25. Myhra converted and NDU led 14-13.

The score stayed that way through the third period although Augie once got to the NDU 9 before Howlin fumbled and Grumbo recovered.

Augustana grabbed the lead with nine minutes left when Nelson bucked straight ahead to score from the one. The Vikings had driven from their own 21.

Chuck Berdahl, sophomore tackle from Garretson, recovered a Sioux bobble on the Augie 45 and Augie's drive began again.

Howlin cut loose for 10, Feiock raced for 20 more as Howlin cut down Piasecki with a perfect block. Howlin then ran 20 more to score on the next play. Nelson's conversion was good and it was 26-14.

Augie was back knocking again at the final horn with the ball on the Sioux 24.

End of a fabulous year

....

If you can force your heart and nerve and sinew to serve your turn long after they are gone, and so hold on when there is nothing in you except the Will which says to them: "Hold on";

If you can fill the unforgiving minute with sixty seconds' worth of distance run—Yours is the Earth and everything that's in it,

AND—WHICH IS MORE—YOU'LL BE A MAN, MY SON.

Rudyard Kipling

....

The Augustana rushing record of 238 yards by Chuck Howlin was not broken until October 1990 when Chris San Agustin rushed for 290 yards in the South Dakota State game.

The conference season of 1956 proved that Augustana could compete with and win games in the North Central Conference. The many years of 'drought' had finally been brought to an end by the 'Burnsmen'. The seasoned players were the determining point in that successful season. The team did not trounce the other teams, but they did win. Many times the one or two-point margin was due to the coolness of quarterback Phil Nelson and his line of experienced players that could hold the opponent until the play was executed. That steadiness was the key to the year. The Augie players did not lose their 'cool' at any crucial time.

The Augustana team of 1956 achieved so many 'firsts' that year that it surely was one of the greatest seasons in Augie's football history. Predicted to finish last, then to climb to the top conference game to determine the season's conference championship was a phenomenal achievement. Football records were set that would take years to surpass. Determined players like Dick Fredricks, Bob Newcomb, Ken Richards, Terry Hokenstad and Carl Guthals kept the fans and supporters of Augustana behind them the complete year. Their sixty-minutes of play week after week was commendable.

These Augie seniors had proved to themselves and their fans that Augustana could compete and win in football.

Lack of injuries to these key players could be attributed to their mental and physical training and to good luck. They were winners in every sense of the word. To go from last to almost first was a greater feat than being second or third and then finishing in the lead. The climb to football respectability in 1956 by the Burnsmen was a achievement that all of the Heartland will long remember.

A final game lost against Lincoln University, played in Missouri, did not dampen the feeling of the Sioux Falls community. Augie was picked to lose by sixty points. Augie lost by one touchdown. The game could just as well have been canceled as the Vikings had just completed their most successful season in South Dakota.

This 1956 football team had produced a most successful Conference season for Augie. More importantly it lifted the school spirit on the entire Augustana campus. Coach Burns' six seasons with Augustana continued to stir up interest and excitement for the school and the Heartland every time a game was played. He was an extraordinary coach.

The season of '56 was a good season for me. I felt I had completed my athletic career successfully and I had gone out a winner. I was to find out that it was a short-lived sensation. Unfortunately I was to experience a let-down after graduation. The economy was in a recession and my services were not in demand in my own hometown. I was ready for the world, but the world was not ready for me. I found temporary employment at the post office carrying mail. In January, 1958, I got married and the next day my wife and I left for Colorado to continue our education. Eventually we found employment in California. I have always felt it ironic that the Heartland gave me my education, and I then had to leave in order to use the gift that the people of Sioux Falls had paid for.

Gordon Jim Wayne 'Butch' Spars • Edith Spear • Beulah Davis Spielman • Gloria Spiering • Linda Stabbe • Leroy Stadem • Charles Stadfeld • Ann Stahlheim • Daniel Jimmy Pat Virginia Sally Mary Loretta Vosika Bill Francis Stanton • Dick Steve Stub Mildred Starns • Mark David Stavig • Marlon Stearns • Bud Montie Babe Dolly Stearns • Solveig Steen • Robert Steensma • William Jr Steever • Dannis Steffen • June Stene • Ruth Stenseth • Ellen Engles Basche Stephenson • Mae Lou Stephenson • Dale Stoakes • Audene Stoeveken • Lois Stokke • Charles Stoneback • Doris Shurmer Stoops • Galen Stoops • Charles Storslee • Wayne Stoutenberg • Rolland Stuckey • Shelley Rose Stutson • Douglas Sugrue • Judy Swanson • Carol Swartz • Lorna Swift • Carol Tripp Symens • Don Tastad • Gerald Teslow • Mark Thelin • James Thissell • Beverly Thomas • Bud Thoms • Phyllis Thompson • Marlene Thomsen • Kenneth Tiahrt • Brenton Tilden • Dennis Tippett • Betty Torkelson • Ann Trandal • Ray Trickey • Marcella Tripp • Mary Tuenge • Paul Harold Harry Marv Bernard Don 'Speed' Rob Tunge • Bob Twedt • John Turner • Betty Hoefer Twedt • Russell Twedt • William Ruth Cora Williams Mary Nesheim 'Bud' Bob Betty Dorothy James Joyce Norma Donna George Tyler • Carol Udseth • Marlene Unverzagt • James Unzicker • Rod Upton • Gloria Keep Urban • Dorothy Van der Meer • Bernice Verch • Ronald Van Wyhe • Lois Vosacek • Ronald Vosacek • Jervin Wait • Cathy Walker • Adam Robert Walker • Duane Wardell • Shirley Wardell • Betty Walsh • Bob Karen Cummings Walton • Gerald Warren • Shirley Wassink • Dwane Watson • Rodney Watson • Robert Weber • Ted Weber • Gary Wehlage • Jeanne Weir • Morton Weiss • John Wells • Robert Wells • James Welbourne • Jim Norm Wesby • Joyce West • Bill Westerdahl • Ann Wheeldon • Leora Ostrosky Whaley • Dolores Whitcomb • Connie White • Chester Whitney • Jackie Wickersham • Bob Vikander • Gerald Gary John Wilcox • Paul Willadson • Jacqueline Williams • Joyce Williams • LaBelle Wilson • Shirley Wilson • Charles Wilson • Milo Winter • Marlene Winters • Marlys Dahl Wipf • James Wissert • Don Wolf • Delores Jacobson Woldt • Carol Wordelman • Dennis Wright • Leland Wylie • Delores Wyrick • Mary Young • Andy Zephier • Leo Zeuger • Barbara Zimmerman • Gretchen Zimmerman • Margaret Zimmerman • Bill Ziske • Joan Zorn • Dick Peg Kim Karol Fredricks • Bob Karol Mathew Gallucci • Joe Kim Amanda Lauren Meyer

11
Return to California

The room was still very dark as I fumbled around in the living room to find the alarm clock. Instinctively I knew it was almost time to get up. Actually I had already been stirred out of my slumber by someone walking across the far side of the room. It was my sister getting up to make coffee. She had closed the door to the kitchen, but a little streak of light was visible, enabling me to find the clock. It was close to six o'clock. No need to rush, the plane didn't leave until after eight o'clock.

Sitting up in the pull-out bed with a pillow propped behind me, my mind started drifting back to the neighborhood where I grew up—Galesburg. The reunion that I had attended a few days ago had been a day full of great fun and excitement that had come to an end too soon. For me, this had been an exhilarating experience to meet many of my old buddies. Surprisingly the crowd was larger than I expected. It had been a cold afternoon. More than sixty people who had grown up in the Galesburg neighborhood passed through the doors of the American Legion. This reunion had become so popular over the years that people who were not able to attend continued to send donations from all parts of the country to help some kids go to Y.M.C.A. camp. Several hundred dollars had been collected for this cause. As in past years, a number of 'regulars'—the Nashs, Harveys, Engles, Mongers, Lehmans, Tunges, Shafer, Hanson, Westby, Stoop, etc., etc., etc., attended and they too had donated to keep this tradition alive.

Finally the smell of fresh coffee became too tempting and, after dressing and making the bed, I went into the kitchen and poured myself a cup.

Departure

Elevation of Sioux Falls 1200 feet, the sign on the airport wall informed me. The 8:15 A.M. flight of the Delta plane had to wait on the runway for only a few minutes before we took off. The sudden acceleration of the jet engines pushed everyone back into their seats. As we rapidly gained altitude, the airport and runways seemed to shrink. The vast checkerboard pattern of the fields below us came into view and as the plane banked for a left turn. The city of Sioux Falls again came into our sights like a miniature toy town on a game board. The twenty-foot tall quartzite stone, Pioneer Monument, pointed itself out to me. The water of the meandering Sioux River glistened like a silver snake on the ground. The plane quickly passed over the Arena and sports complex and then over the enormous holes of the quartzite stone quarries of West Sioux Falls. The quarries were reduced to dots as the plane continued to climb. Tank Town was passed and the notorious Skunk Creek, whose waters had contributed to many a flood in the Sioux Valley, came into

The Galesburg Gang. Far back: Lenard Burben, Lee Lehman and Bob Walker. Third Row: John Irish, Gordon Spars, Wayne Spars, Don Spars, Norm Small, Don Wesby, Skadsen, English, Bob Johnson, Lee Harvey Bernie Tunge, Ronnie Fisher, Ray Engels, Speed Tunge, Hank Sachen, Bert Fonter, Chub Shafer, Dick Neish and Larry Monger. Second Row: Tim Nash, Sam Nash, Don Butts, Bill Polzien, Clayton Scott, Bill Ziske, Swanson, John Eich, Rich Rose, Jim Wesby and Dick Fredricks. Front Row: Dick Kinney, Jervin Wait, Galen Stoops, Bill Ranney, Tom Hanson, Chuck Sachen and 'Snook' Anderson.

140

view. The plane then passed the tiny burg of Tea and was now to the west of the community of Chancellor. We continued to gain altitude and began heading due west. On the ground numerous water ponds that the glaciers had gouged out in the last Ice Age reflected the sun and blinded the view of the surrounding towns. Everything below was becoming a blur now. The plane seemed to be moving more slowly, but this was only an illusion of flying as the plane increased its elevation to over 30,000 feet, six miles from the ground. Suddenly a white cloud puffed by the window of the plane, then another, and another, and the plane shook violently as we hit a bit of turbulence. I glanced up to the panel in front of me and took notice of the 'Seat belt' sign that was still lit up. All of a sudden I could see nothing but a bright white sky out of the window. I leaned back into my seat and relaxed. The ground was no longer visible. Slowly I became drowsy. Finally I slept, dreaming of my memorable stay in the heart of the continent.

A look back

In addition to attending the Galesburg reunion, a number of other pleasant events happened to me on this visit. One of the most important events was renewing my contact with a former WHS student and fellow Augieite, Stan Cadwell. I had visited the Pine Hill Press in Freeman to inquire about a book on California history I was developing. In the process I acquired a number of local contacts for editing purposes that I might need and in the list was the name of Rushmore House Publishing. On my return to Sioux Falls I contacted Stan Cadwell to gain more information. He encouraged me to gather my vignettes, rewrite them, and consider publishing them at Pine Hill Press. After leaving Sioux Falls I called Stan a number of times and after a year I felt I was close to having a publication ready. I was ready to print, but not ready to finance. Another six months passed before, in 1999, I decided to go ahead with the project. During a visit to Sioux Falls, I had heard from someone that there was a big Washington High School reunion in the works. I contacted Windy Elliott and Dick Erickson to check out the rumor, and they confirmed that there was to be a reunion in July 2000. Perfect. That was to be my excuse to take the risk of putting my own money into a publication of this book. Out of these conversations came my publication of the book about life in the Heartland during the 1930s and '40s called *When Lilacs were in Bloom*.

The reception after the publication of the book in November 1999 was so gratifying. I never in my wildest dreams had believed that it would be so well received and be so successful. The stories in the book about my twenty-five years in Sioux Falls had hit many a familiar chord in the hearts of former classmates and acquaintances. The WHS reunion in July 2000 reaffirmed my feelings that the memories I had recorded in the 'Lilacs' book were only the tip of the iceberg. I had concluded the book too soon. It ended with my final days at WHS without covering the next big influence in my life, the 1950s and my experiences at Augustana College and in the Army. The 1950s were a beginning of many great changes in Sioux Falls and the Heartland. The changes would transform the physical aspect of the city greatly, but also it would change the Heartland's outlook and personality. It seems that much of the feeling of togetherness and of the pride that we took in our homeland was being challenged. During the 1950s my life was in a great transition also. That part of my life in Sioux Falls seemed like an up-and-down elevator of emotion. History books are great for telling about the buildings of a community, but they often leave out the struggles of the real people who have infused life into the community. Coach Burns and the 'Cinderella' Augustana football team of 1956 rejuvenated life and breathed a breath of fresh air into the community. I needed to relate these changes in 'our town' and the Heartland to the many hundreds of people who had read When Lilacs were in Bloom...and who remembered these yesterdays along with me.

Thus began the book I now call Lilacs two—The 1950's.

I hope It seems like yesterday—*Lilacs two—The 1950's* is as well received in the Heartland as was *When Lilacs were in Bloom.*

Coach Bob Burns died Monday November 6, 2000.

Augie Memories

Kent Morsted, Dean Forbard, Chuck Howlin, Bob Bittner, Jon Falgren and Ordell.

Bob Newcomb, Joe Fenstermacher, Bob Bittner, Dick Jensen and Bob Moe.

*Left: Dow Drug 26th and Minnesota,
Below: Park Ridge Barber Shop*

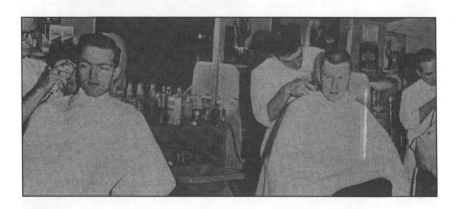

Larry, Dick Boetcher, Bill Dickey and Jim Oujes.

Maryln Graff, Jim Howlin, and Evelyn Fodness.

Grace and Joloyce.

2605 West 12th.

The Barrell

Walt and Mary's.

President and Mrs. L.M. Stavig.

212 North Phillips.

31st and Minnesota.

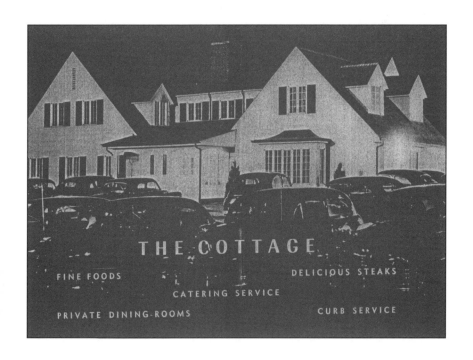

Photo Credits

I greatly appreciate the cooporation of Augustana College, The Center for Western Studies, Gary Olson and Joel Strasser for allowing me to use these photographs and illustrations.

Order Form

TO PLACE AN ORDER:			
Quantity	Description	Price Each	Total
	Lilacs two — the 1950s	$12.95	
	When Lilacs were in Bloom the 30s and 40s	$12.95	
	Both Books (Publishers Special)	$22.00	
	Shipping and Handling	$3.00	
	GRAND TOTAL		

Name: _____

Address: _____

City_____ State _____ Zip Code _____

Phone: _____

Send check or money order to:

Darold Fredricks
P.O. Box 733
San Bruno, CA 94066